REFLECTIONS ON MONOTHEISM

THE SEED

AND

THE SPERM

by

**Muhammad Abbas Nadeem
Al Shareef**

Ta-Ha Publishers Ltd.
1, Wynne Road
London SW9 0BB

Published by

Ta-Ha Publishers Ltd.
1 Wynne Road
London SW9 0BB

By: Muhammad Abbas Nadeem Al-Shareef

Edited by: Abdassamad Clarke

British Library Cataloguing in Publication Data
Nadeem, Muhammad Abbas
The Seed and the Sperm
I. Title

ISBN: 1-897940-12-2

Typeset by: BookWright, The Isle of Lewis.
Tel:0851-870198.
Printed by: Deluxe Printers, London.
Tel: 081-965 1771

Table of Contents

INTRODUCTION

Repair Without Despair

All praise belongs to Allah, the Exalted, who made me a Muslim, and praise and thanks are due to Him for His goodness to me which is uncountable except by Him alone. I love purity of faith, of belief, and love God (Allah) most, His prophets, messengers, and the last of the prophets, Muhammad, *salla'llahu alaihi wa sallam.*

The only 'peaceful solution' to all the miseries of the human race, until the Last Day, is for us to have belief and trust in Allah and in His Messengers, the last of whom is the prophet Muhammad, *salla'llahu alaihi wa sallam.* "There is for you in the Messenger of Allah a beautiful example ..." (Qur'an 33: 21). He is the perfect exemplar for all mankind, "... a mercy for all creatures". (Qur'an 21: 107). "Whoever obeys the Messenger has obeyed Allah." (Qur'an 4: 80). We achieve that obedience by embodying the Qur'an and the Sunnah, the customary practice of the Prophet, *salla'llahu alaihi wa sallam,* in governance as well as in personal behaviour.

After the historical prophethood of Muhammad, *salla'llahu alaihi wa sallam,* Islam is the only way of life and of worship acceptable to Allah. "Whoever desires other than Islam (submission to Allah) as a religion, then it will never be accepted from him and he, in the next life, will be one of the losers." (Qur'an 3: 85). If we really do trust in Allah, we should obey Him, trust in His revealed books the last of which is the Qur'an and we should make no distinction between His prophets and messengers. Their message to all people is to worship Allah, the One, who has no equals, no partners and that we should associate nothing with Him.

"Say, 'He, Allah, is one. Allah is the Eternally Besought of all. He did not give birth and He was not born. And there is none equal to Him.'"

(Qur'an, Al-Ikhlas [or Sincerity]: 1-4).

As we know that we should obey Allah, with no other alternative than to obey Him, then clearly we must believe in all His prophets and messengers, in submission to His orders.

The Qur'an is the last revealed book for the human race. Muhammad, *salla'llahu alaihi wa sallam*, is the seal of all the prophets sent to mankind regardless of their creed, race or colour. He is "... the Messenger of Allah and the Seal of the Prophets".

(Qur'an, The Confederates: 40).

"Say, 'O mankind, I am the Messenger of Allah to you all, of Him to whom belongs the kingdom of the heavens and the earth. There is no god but He. He gives life and causes to die. So believe in Allah and His Messenger, the unlettered Prophet who believes in Allah and His words, and follow him that you may be led correctly.'"

(Qur'an, Al-Araf: 158).

People read the latest issues of books, journals, newspapers, etc., and officials look to the latest office circulars to up-date their information. Allah's last revelation, in which He gives us the latest news, information, commandments and prohibitions, is the Qur'an.

It is only logical that we should submit to Him, by means of His last revelation, being His slaves and subjects, created by Him, and because we are returning to Him. This is complete submission to Allah, the Exalted, the Owner of the heavens and the earth and all that is in between them and we Muslims thankfully submit to Him. We witness that there is no god but Allah and that Muhammad is the Messenger of Allah – *Laa ilaaha illa'llah, Muhammad Rasoulu'llah*. All praise belongs to Allah.

If we had been living in the time of Isa (Jesus), *alaihi's-salaam*, before the prophethood of Muhammad, *salla'llahu alaihi wa sallam*, we would have said, "There is no god but Allah and Isa is the Messenger of Allah". Similarly during the messengerships of all the other Messengers right back to Nuh (Noah), those of them we know and those we don't know, *alaihimu's-salaam*. The last prophet conveyed to us the most recent information concerning worship, purity of faith, conduct and rule. Arrogance is from Shaytan driving some people from the right path and leading them to the Fire. "Say, 'O mankind, I am the Messenger of Allah to you all, of Him to whom belongs the kingdom of the heavens and the earth. There is no god but He. He gives life and causes to die. So believe in Allah and His Messenger, the unlettered Prophet who believes in Allah and His words, and follow him that you may be led correctly.'"

(Qur'an, Al-Araf: 158).

The Seed and the Sperm

Many people may abstain from accepting Islam making as an excuse the bad deeds of some of the Muslims. This is not correct thinking. The highest and noblest model for people to follow and the one permitted by Allah is that of the Prophet Muhammad, *salla'llahu alaihi wa sallam*. Allah, the Exalted, says, "There is for you in the Messenger of Allah a beautiful example for whoever hopes for Allah and the Last Day and remembers Allah a great deal."

Those who have a high rank in following the Qur'an and the Sunnah are among the highest and most exalted of the believers and of the Muslims. Others, who have lesser achievement in following them, are at a lower level. Some others need to repent to Allah of their bad conduct lest they be driven from Allah's mercy and punished in the Fire. Those of the first degree will abide in Paradise with the prophets and the believers.

Allah says, "Whoever obeys Allah and the Messenger then those are with the ones whom Allah has blessed of the prophets and the completely sincere ones, the martyrs and the righteous (those who do good). Those are beautiful as a company."

(Qur'an, The Women: 69).

The gates of Allah's mercy are open to all people, to turn towards Him from their disbelief and their wrong actions, to redress the wrongs they have done and to go forward on the right path. "Why do they not turn towards Allah and seek His forgiveness? For Allah is most forgiving, most merciful."

(Qur'an, The Table: 74).

We are, *insha'Allah*, going to address some matters that are in the Qur'an, the last revelation from the Divine;

which perhaps a good many non-Muslims have never read. It is no excuse on the Last Day to plead ignorance. Yet whatsoever one has committed of mistakes, or however much one has gone astray, once one has repented, Allah will forgive one. Consequently one starts afresh on the right path.

The upheaval caused by scientific discoveries is characteristic of this age. It is the age of the information explosion and of new technologies. What it lacks is a genuine knowledge of the Creator, His true worship and consequent harmonious way of living, which is Islam. The Creator has chosen this way of Islam for all mankind. "This day, I have perfected your religion for you and completed My favour upon you and I am pleased for you to have Islam as a religion."
(Qur'an, The Table: 3).

If we were to add Islam to this age's achievements it would indeed be a remarkable age.

To deepen our conviction of the presence of Allah we look upon, contemplate and reflect on His creation. These reflections deepen our certainty. The seed and the sperm, the subjects of this book are two examples. We belong to the creed of our father Ibrahim, *alaihi's-salaam*, as well as to the way of our Prophet Muhammad, *salla'llahu alaihi wa sallam*, who both fought idolatry.

"Ibrahim said to his father Azar, 'Do you take idols as gods? I see you and your people in clear error.' So also did we show Ibrahim the kingdom of the heavens and the earth that he might be among those who have deep certainty. When the night covered him, he saw a star. He said, 'This is my Lord,' but when it set he said,

The Seed and the Sperm

'I love not those that set.' When he saw the moon rising in splendour he said, 'This is my Lord.' But when the moon set he said, 'Unless my Lord guides me I shall surely be among those who go astray.' When he saw the sun rising in splendour he said, 'This is my Lord, this is greater.' Then when it set he said, 'O my people, I am indeed free from all that you associate (as partners with Allah). I have set my face towards the One who created the heavens and the earth. And I am not one of those who associate (others as partners with Allah).'"

(Qur'an, Cattle: 74-79).

Through his contemplation of the creation and his pleading to Allah to lead him to the right path and not to let him be among the losers, he then saw clearly that Allah is the Truth and that He is Omnipotent. Allah guided him to the right path; that there is only Allah, one god, and He has no partners. He became disgusted with what his people used to worship. This resulted in a deeper conviction and an unshakeable faith. This is an example of gaining a deep conviction by pondering Allah's creation.

Those who specialise in the studies of biology, anatomy, physiology, botany, physics, astronomy, chemistry, the applied sciences, etc., should look deeply to understand clearly the marvels of creation and realise the impossibility of its being produced spontaneously or out of a vacuum. If they did that they would come to the recognition of unity in the creation and to realise that Allah, who created the heavens and the earth, is One. That is the sole purpose of learning. Our target in life is, believing in Allah, to come to put our trust in Him, worship Him and to make all our actions in harmony with that. Allah the Exalted says, "I did not create Jinn and mankind except that they should worship Me."

(Qur'an 51: 56).

Indeed there is no god but He, the One and only God. If there are other gods, then let them create another moon, another heaven, or wipe out the sun from existence. There is no god but He, the only God, our Creator, Beneficent Master and All-Merciful Lord. If He had partners, the universe would have perished by their conflicts.

"Allah has not taken to Himself any son nor is there any god along with Him; for then each god would have gone off with that which he had created, and some of them would have risen up over others; glory be to Allah beyond that which they ascribe."

(Qur'an, The Believers: 91).

Since Allah created the worlds, the heavens and the earth, the moon, the sun and the oceans, then they tell the reflective being of His all-pervading presence and His all-inclusive knowledge.

All provision and sustenance is from Him alone; none of it is from anyone else. "And in the heaven there is your provision (sustenance), and that which you are promised."

(Qur'an 51: 22).

With conviction and trust the road to Paradise is paved, and with disbelief and distrust the road to the Fire is paved and its gates are wide open awaiting those who disbelieve. Sceptre and crown tumble down eventually. Neither the prophets nor the believers are in any sense His partners. He, alone, is the King with His permanence and His grandeur.

"We said, 'Get down from it (paradise), all of you; and if, as is sure, there comes to you guidance from Me, then whosoever follows My guidance there is no fear on them, neither shall they grieve."

(Qur'an, 2: 38).

The last revealed book, the Qur'an, and the Sunnah, the customary practice of His Messenger Muhammad, *salla'llahu alaihi wa sallam* contain the last guidance to humanity, as Allah has promised. The only peaceful solution to all the distress and woes of mankind is to follow these two. We believe, we obey and we plead with Allah to forgive us our wrong actions. I ask Allah, the Exalted, to accept my effort, for His sake, and to make it a fruitful work for me and for many others. I earnestly Him to guide us and all humanity to the right path which He has blessed.

THE QUR'AN AND SUNNAH
Must be Taught World-wide

I think that the lack of teaching of Islam, in most educational institutions, school and universities, is a great misfortune and the cause of a real failure in proper education. Particularly grave is the situation regarding the teaching of the Qur'an and the Sunnah. The knowledge of them, if Allah wills, brings people into the light of truth. That would be for them precious and valuable beyond their wildest imaginings. Universities appear to be edifices of instruction. The degrees awarded therein give graduates the sense of being the cream of creation. They also qualify them for senior positions in society. Graduates hardly realise that they have missed the most vital part of knowledge, that knowledge of the *deen* (religion) which is a light illuminating everything else they study. That is better than their learning blindly and staggering on in complete darkness. The weapons of knowledge that they have acquired turn against them and against humanity at large. The reality is that lack of knowledge of Qur'an and Sunnah is ignorance itself. Ignorance is an enemy indeed and is the best weapon that Shaytan (Satan, the Devil) has, because the ignorant man is an easy prey for him.

The first revelation to the Prophet Muhammad, *salla'llahu alaihi wa sallam*, was, "Read! (recite!) in the name of your Lord who created. He created the human being from a blood-clot. Read! And your Lord and Cherisher is the Most Generous who taught by the pen, taught man what he did not know."

(Qur'an 96: 1-5).

He, *salla'llahu alaihi wa sallam*, was taught the Qur'an, and the laws of behaviour, worship and wisdom. It is not something personal and private but a mercy to all mankind. Lack of it is impoverishment of all good. Gaining it is light in this life and after death. Without it one remains as void of humanity as a machine except that when a human machine breaks down finally its end is the Fire.

Some in the modern age have drifted far away from this guidance. This may be due to a contorted theology and biblical texts, the Old Testament and the New Testament which are full of contradictions due to man-made changes in what were originally true revelations

The Seed and the Sperm

from Allah, the Torah and the Gospel. Allah revealed this criminal act, their altering the divinely revealed books, in the Qur'an (see Qur'an 2: 75, 79: 3-78). Actually there is no more serious crime whatever may be its degree than altering a revelation and thus misleading countless people until the Last Day. It is indeed a horrible act. Nowadays, if one changed a legal document issued by a court one would be held as a criminal for committing a forgery. What comparison can there be with changing a revelation from Allah? A revelation is the most vital thing in the lives of mankind. It concerns their ultimate destiny in the Fire or the Garden. So this crime has no equivalent. Allah is the highest witness, and the angels, the believers, and those whom Allah has given knowledge are also witnesses.

Allah, the Exalted says, "And truly there is a party of them who twist their tongues with the Book, that you may suppose it part of the Book, yet it is not part of the Book, and they say, 'It is from Allah,' and it is not from Allah and they speak a lie against Allah and they know."

(Qur'an 3: 78).

Allah says, "Are you all then so eager that they will believe you, yet a party of them used to listen to the speech of Allah and then they would pervert it after they had grasped it, knowingly."

(Qur'an 2: 75).

He also says, "So woe to those who write the Book with their hands and then say, 'This is from Allah,' that they may sell it for a little price. So woe to them from what their hands have written and woe to them from what they earn." (Qur'an 2: 79).

16

It is the most disgraceful act to dare to change the Speech of Allah and to allege that Isa, *alaihi's-salaam*, is god, or the son of god, or that Uzair is the son of god, or that god is a trinity. Glory be to the Almighty, the Great, High and Exalted beyond what they ascribe.

(See Qur'an 5: 17, 72, 73; 9: 30).

All my effort in this book will be to show the greatness of the Creator and His exaltation beyond what they attribute because I find their fraud to be shameful, their crime to be abhorrent.

Allah, the Exalted, says, "They have certainly disbelieved those who say, 'Allah is the Messiah the son of Maryam.'"

(Qur'an 5: 17).

"They have disbelieved those who say, 'Allah is the Messiah the son of Maryam,' for the Messiah said, 'O Children of Israel, worship Allah, my Lord and your Lord. Truly, whoever associates as partner anything with Allah, then Allah will prohibit him entrance to the garden, and his refuge will be the Fire. And wrong-doers have no helpers.'"

(Qur'an 5: 72).

"They have disbelieved those who say, 'Allah is the third of three.' There is no god but Allah. If they do not refrain from what they say, there shall afflict those of them who disbelieve a painful torment."

(Qur'an 5: 73).

"And the Jews say, 'Uzair is the son of Allah.' The Christians say, 'The Messiah is the son of Allah.' That is their sayings with their mouths, conforming with those who disbelieved before them. Allah has cursed them; how perverted they are." (Qur'an 9: 30).

The Seed and the Sperm

After the enormity of the crime, Allah extends His mercy to those who turn away from their wrong action and turn penitent to Him, "Will they not turn to Allah and seek His forgiveness? Truly Allah is all-forgiving, all-compassionate."
(Qur'an 5: 74).

These matters are very serious and vital to man, both in this life and especially in the life after death. The condition of modern non-Muslim man is that they doubt because they have inherited and been taught a perverted creed. Most have become disillusioned and have turned away from 'religion'. They look with suspicion at their 'religion', neither daring to abandon it totally, nor able to rest in it in peace. With heavy hearts they prefer to transfer their interest and their spirit of enquiry to other spheres, science, technology, experimentation, ordinary human experience, and to narrow specialisations, to have a better grasp of life.

This abandoning of a perverted religion has led to the growth of other creeds and groups such as scientology, psychonomic science, sociology and different forms of governance and a plethora of philosophies. People have wandered far from the simple and clear path of Allah, confused by degrees, certificates of education, diplomas and doctorates, most of which veil the true way, the true religion and the true 'religion'. Some, lacking proper and thorough knowledge, take science as a creed, as a cult, with which they try to solve mankind's problems (Scientology[1]). Some have taken sciences that concern themselves with human behaviour (psychonomic sciences) as a creed, as a religion, more or less. To take science as a creed or a cult or a religion is a deviation from the clear and simple right path of Allah and complete loss. It is only sensible to measure scientific *facts* in the light of the word of God, to see how these *facts* are reasonable and valid. It is in this way that several authors[2,3,4] and I have dealt with some findings, as I hope to show in the following.

I have stressed certain points to affirm that all knowledge is from Allah, the All-Knowing. He says, "And you have not been given of knowledge but a little." (Qur'an 17: 85). He, the Exalted, gave details of knowledge of the revelation to certain people, mainly the prophets, as well as giving the details of certain knowledge such as mathematics, botany, biology, astronomy, etc., to others. The knowledge given to prophets and Messengers of Allah, the last of whom is the Seal of the Prophets, is revelation. It is exact whereas other knowledge always needs research, observation, evaluation and verification. I have chosen one case of reproduction studied by a biologist who had no idea of any religion or the Qur'an. I compared the scientific description of the process with statements in the Qur'an concerning human reproduction (see Qur'an 22: 5). It is amazing to see that the main steps in the process of reproduction are the same in both. I compared it with some statements of the Prophet Muhammad, *salla'llahu alaihi wa sallam*, and found again the same agreement. Furthermore, I found knowledge in the sayings of the Prophet, *salla'llahu alaihi wa sallam*, which scientific research has not reached. One of the sayings of the Prophet, *salla'llahu alaihi wa sallam*, on genetics and on what determines the gender of the baby was identical to the findings of scientific research.

The Seed and the Sperm

It is beyond doubt that all types of knowledge come from Allah, the Almighty, the Originator, the Designer, the Creator and the All-Knowing. He guides and misleads as He wills, and according to His infinite knowledge of His creation. The most dangerous types of knowledge and the ones most likely to mislead are the theoretical philosophy of behaviour and the man-made philosophies that are designed for people who are astray. They are left to ramble in strange dark avenues of thought, unless they turn back to Allah.

One lecturer I know of gave a lecture on a university platform under the banner of "The Freedom of Sex" hiding behind his doctoral qualifications, defining marriage as an agreement, legal or not, among people, to live together, many men having one wife or a number of wives, under one roof. He thought that no form of polyandry need be considered illegal. He didn't consider revelation. Everything that Allah prohibited, in every revelation given to mankind, he considered permitted. Allah, the Patient, is All-Powerful. He does not guide wrong-doers, who disbelieve, to the light.

Allah, the Exalted, says, "Those who disbelieve and act unjustly, Allah would not forgive them, nor guide them on any path except the path to Jahannam, therein abiding for ever. That is easy for Allah."
(Qur'an 4: 168-169).

"Allah strengthens the ones who believe with the firm saying in the present life and in the next life. And Allah misleads unjust wrongdoers. And Allah does what He wills." (Qur'an 14: 27).

The above *ayats*, (sign, and verses) which refer to the misguidance of wrongdoers, govern most of the social and psychonomic sciences (which refer to laws or principles of behaviour). Without the guidance of Allah such fields of knowledge are those which people are most likely to stray into, i.e. go astray from the clear path of Allah. These studies are from man's limited mental capacities and are not based on revelation. For this reason it is criminal to teach them universally as though they were undisputed truth. Almost all psychopathic problems are due to; a lack of true knowledge of Allah, bad conduct and ignorance of the *deen*: "Farel discovered a number of gaps in the literature of religion. He wrote, 'We have very little information about how beliefs and values develop, and how religious organisations influence religious development. We don't know how religion enhances self-control, if it does at all. We have no consensus on definitions used to describe religion. WE NEED MORE RESEARCH INTO THE RELATIONSHIP BETWEEN THE SOCIAL CONTEXT AND RELIGIOUS DEVELOPMENT. We are not certain of the relationship, if any, between religious faith and religious practice.'"[5]

Even the meagre religious knowledge men like this have, leads them astray from true knowledge and the trust which springs from it. Religion is not by consensus. It is, first and last, by purity of trust in Allah and in the revelations to the prophets and messengers of Allah. The social and religious aspects of Islam are one homogeneous identity.

"Fowler believes that faith, which he defines as patterns of thinking that motivate behaviour, is the basis of the struggle to find meaning in life." That is perfectly true, if 'faith' is known aright, but unfortunately cognition is astray:

Some children (aged 6-11) "enjoy ritual and music, perceive God (in human form), and ask no questions concerning the beliefs and rules of religion's heritage."[6] This is of course an abhorrent and wrongful conception, and is part of a bad upbringing. It is entirely due to the failure of parents to impart any meaningful conception of Divinity. Allah is great and sublime, glorious and exalted, and cannot be imagined in any human form or image. That is an absurd thought.

He continues that others of the ages 12-18 "conceive of a less personalised God, but one who is something of a personal adviser and guide."[7] The same deviated conception evolves to higher stages in adolescence. He finds that some at the age (of 18 or over), which is the beginning of the stage of adulthood, believe that, "God is not a personal adviser, but an abstract concept embodying moral truth."[8] This is far from the truth. Allah is the reality and not an abstract in any sense. Glory be to Allah, high is He exalted above what they ascribe. It is all poor upbringing and wrong teaching of the nature of faith and religion, which are the most vital things to the human being.

I have tried in this book to deal seriously with this idea of abstractness, and to emphasise the tangible reality and eternal presence of Allah. I hope it serves this purpose to wash away every obscurity in this matter.

What I hope indeed, is that as long as anyone is seeking the truth by every possible means, including academic ones, to arrive at real knowledge, they may be saved and with open heart see the truth clearly and stick to it. We are, by His express command, to convey the truth clearly, as we have read His last revelation, the Qur'an. It is the command of Allah that we convey the truth to people as much as we can. Allah says, "Those who conceal that which We have revealed of the clear explaining signs and of the guidance after We have made it clear to people in the Book, those Allah curses and there curse them those who curse."

(Qur'an 2: 159).

It must be clear to anybody who hopes for safety from Allah's punishment and from the Fire on the Last Day, that there is no alternative to Islam, which is surrender and submission to the will of Allah. Islam is the beginning and the end. It begins with Nuh and continues with Ibrahim, Musa, Isa and the last prophet and messenger of Allah, Muhammad, *salla'llahu alaihi wa sallam*, and it is, in this age, to declare that, "There is no god but Allah" – *Laa ilaaha illa'llah*, and that "Muhammad is the Messenger of Allah" – *Muhammad Rasoulu'llah*; It is to recognise that He, Allah, is One. Allah is the Eternal, the Absolute, the Besought of all. He does not give birth, nor is He born, and He has no equal, nor partner.

The Prophet Muhammad, *salla'llahu alaihi wa sallam*, sent an envoy to Heraclius, the Emperor of Rome, inviting him to submit to Allah.[9] Allah ordered him to convey the following: "'O people of the Book, come to common terms between us and you, that we worship none but Allah, that we associate nothing with Him as a partner, that we take not from among ourselves Lords apart from Allah'. If they turn their backs then say, 'Witness that we are Muslims (submitted to Allah).'"

(Qur'an, Ali Imran: 64).

The Seed and the Sperm

Submission to Allah (Islam) is not new. Nuh asked his people to submit to Allah, to obey him, to worship Allah alone and seek His forgiveness. That was the same message of all the prophets, submission to Allah (Islam); the message of Ibrahim, Ismail, Ishaq, Yaqoub, Musa and Isa, *alaihimu's-salaam*, and the last of the prophets, Muhammad, *salla'llahu alaihi wa sallam*.

"Say, 'We believe inAllah, and in that which was revealed to us, and in that which was revealed to Ibrahim, Ismail, Ishaq, Yaqoub, and the tribes, and that which Musa and Isa and the prophets received from their Lord, we make no distinction between any of them and we are submitted (Muslims) to Him.' And if they believe in the like of that which you believe in, then they have been guided. And if they turn away, then they are clearly in schism; so Allah will suffice you against them and He is the All-Hearing, the All-Knowing."

(Qur'an 2: 136-137).

"Whoever desires other than Islam (submission and surrender to Allah) as a religion then it will never be accepted from him and he, in the next life, will be one of the losers."

(Qur'an 3: 85).

Islam is a *deen*, which means that it is a religion, a creed and a mode of behaviour. It has elements of worship, social transaction, psychological wisdom and understanding and teaching on market transactions, trade and agriculture, which are all based on trust in Allah and following the last of His prophets and Messengers, Muhammad, *salla'llahu alaihi wa sallam*, as a model and exemplar. There is no other model for humanity to compare with him. That along with the light that was revealed to him, the Qur'an, and the true knowledge of Allah that he brought, are the elements that can go to make a healthy and balanced human being. Rather than seeking their identity in different aptitudes of the personality, people can draw their inspiration from modelling themselves on the behaviour of the best of creation, *salla'llahu alaihi wa sallam*. (See Qur'an 33: 21). Looking for other examples would be to stray from the right path. Most non-Muslim psychologists attempt to reach a standard model of personality. They are "not yet in a position to agree on a common definition and theory of the nature of personality."[10] By submitting to Allah one finds that there is a simple and clear standard to cleave to oneself and to raise one's children by, and the Creator affirms that standard. Otherwise one withdraws alone with Shaytan. So nebulous for modern man are the issues of personality, morals and character that it has become rather like building sand castles in the air. Only surmise remains and a society where permanent insanity is acceptable. Why does our society not invest all its faculties and energy on research, trying to cure psychopathic patients within the context of the above picture of the human being, the model acccepted by God?

Almost all psycho-pathological problems are due to a lack of true knowledge of Allah and a failure of trust and faith. Some cases are due to bad breeding, and then the poor upbringing of children without imparting to them the true nature of divinity and demanding their obedience to the revealed law. Upbringing, I say unequivocally, must be on the basis of Islam, the Qur'an and the Sunnah, a profound knowledge of which psychiatrists singularly lack. Knowledge of Islam is fundamental. Lack of that knowledge is ignorance itself.

No-one can guarantee scientific interpretation of data to be free from error, except where it is clearly congruent with the statements of Allah. I have taken one example, the case of reproduction, and compared it with *ayats* of the Qur'an. Where the interpretation of data hasn't reached to the truth, we need still more investigation. Where that interpretation agrees with the law of Allah, then the interpretation of the data is ripe fruitful knowledge. The Qur'an normally gives broad facts, and Allah gives the details of knowledge to those whom He wishes to benefit. When some try to expunge the evidence of the Creator, the Originator of all things, from their examination of the origins of things, then it is either sheer wilful blasphemy, or absolute blindness and ignorance. If a promoter of such ideas is one who disbelieves, and if he doesn't return, in repentance, to acknowledge the Divine before his death, everything we know indicates that he is destined for eternal anguish, no matter what titles he collected here on earth.

There is nothing that is spontaneous of itself. For every action there is an actor. Everything returns to the Originator, the Creator, the Designer, the Giver of life and death to everything, Allah the Almighty, all praise and glory be to Him.

It took some scientists centuries to recant from the idea of spontaneous generation that states that living things come from non-living material. Researchers conducted a discussion for hundreds of years, from the middle of the 17th until the second half of the 18th century, when Louis Pasteur reached the conclusion that reproduction of living things comes from living things only.[11] Scientific problems take people centuries of painstaking work, exhaustive discussion, experimentation and verification to reach the statement of what one could call a 'fact'. Sometimes further research even overturns such 'facts'. So has all of this work arrived at the truth, or should they do more research and, if so, what should they use to take their bearings and what guiding light can they use? If they return to the last guidance and wisdom, the light sent down by the All-Knowing, the revelation from the Divine, the Qur'an, they will find concise statements which are lights to pave the way for them on the course they should take. The following, from the Qur'an, are guiding lights concerning creation:

1. "Allah is the Creator of every thing, and He is the Guardian Disposer of all affairs. To Him belong the keys of the heavens and the earth. And those who reject the *ayats* of Allah, it is they who are in loss." (Qur'an 39: 62-63).

2. "Thou make the night to enter into the day, and Thou make the day to enter into the night, and **Thou bringest forth the living from out of the dead and Thou bringest forth the dead from out of the living,** and Thou provide for whomever Thou will without reckoning." (Qur'an 3: 27).

3. "And from water We made every living thing. Will they not believe?" (Qur'an 21: 30).

4. "And He creates what you have no knowledge of." (Qur'an 16: 8).

The Seed and the Sperm

5. "We created you. So what if you do not affirm? Have you considered that which you ejaculate, is it you who create it or are We the creators? We have decreed among you death and We shall not be outstripped from exchanging the likes of you and creating you anew in that you do not know."

(Qur'an 56: 57-61).

6. "Have you considered that which you cultivate, is it you who cause it to grow or are We the cause?"

(Qur'an 56: 63-64).

7. "Have you considered the water, which you drink, did you send it down from the rain clouds or are We the senders down?"

(Qur'an 56: 68-69).

8. "Have you considered the fire, which you kindle, did you make the tree (which supplies the firewood) or are We the makers?"

(Qur'an 56: 71-72).

9. "Glory be to the One who created the pairs, all of them, of that which the earth grows, and of themselves and of that which they do not know."

(Qur'an 36: 36).

10. "His command, when He wills a thing, is only that He says to it 'Be!' And it 'Is'."

(Qur'an 36: 72).

11. "Truly We have created every thing in measure, and Our command is but one (act) like the glance of an eye."

(Qur'an 54: 49-50).

12. "And there is no creature crawling on the earth nor bird flying with its two wings but that they are communities the like of you. We have neglected noth-

ing in the Book. Then to their Lord they are mustered."
(Qur'an 6: 38).

So scientific interpretation is not conclusive. Ages
have passed in discussing spontaneous generation and
whether living things come out of dead things or from
living things; and Allah has stated that He brings forth
the living from the dead and the dead from the living.
Adam was first created by the will of Allah; the command **"Be!"** and he **"Became"** from out of clay. Then
Allah breathed the spirit of life into him. On the other
hand, the seed, e.g. the date-stone, is solid and lifeless. After the farmer puts it into the ground and waters it, then the root emerges and descends into the
earth, and the shoot arises and ascends from out of the
earth, and there is eventually a beautiful date tree.
Allah makes from water, every living thing. This all
tells us that researchers could find interesting point-
ers for their investigations, possibly saving time and
money and much argument, by working alongside the
Qur'an.

Scientific researchers can work, with a profound belief in Allah and His words. Much time and argument
could be saved. I will deal with one example in this
book, on reproduction, stating and comparing the *ayats*
of Qur'an with observed processes. Qur'an is very exact. Moreover it is wisdom, law and worship. It has no
parallel or equivalent in any other revealed book, let
alone humanly authored book.

"Say, 'If the whole of mankind and the Jinn were to
gather together to produce the like of this Qur'an they
could not produce the like of it even if they helped
and supported each other. And We have elaborated for

mankind in this Qur'an every kind of simile. But most of mankind refuse everything but complete ingratitude."

(Qur'an 17: 88-89).

Psychiatry, like most sciences and pseudo-sciences, requires careful revision, sorting through and adaptation to human behaviour. Allah has revealed, in the Qur'an and the Sunnah, the way of behaviour. Just as biology, for example, concerns itself with the study of living bodies, Islam concerns itself with conduct, refining of the self and worship, to perfect the human being. Islam itself, in its last form, is the completion and perfection of the previous revealed ways all of which had one single purpose, which is worship of the Divine, Allah. Allah, the Exalted, says, "I have not created Jinn and mankind except to worship Me." (Qur'an 51: 56). Within that context, the human self and the intellect work well, without deception or treachery. Psychiatry cannot restore that healthy intellect because the context is wrong, and in trying to do so it is directly in contradiction of revelation and the Divine. Psychiatry cannot be independent from the revealed societal law because the shariah is the only way in harmony with the Divine natural law. Psychiatry and the scientific method will inevitably deviate from the truth and lead people astray.

"The history of science teaches us that although we grow up thinking that certain things are right, they often turn out to be otherwise. This is true not only of specific facts, but of whole models of knowledge. The idea that the sun moved around the earth was prevalent for thousands of years, and known to be 'right'.

As new data was perceived (discovered) that failed to fit the old model, a period of crisis began which eventually ended with the Copernican model of the earth moving around the sun.

Thomas Kuhn, in his brilliant monograph, *The Structure of Scientific Revolutions*, analyses such changes in models of scientific thought as they have been found in all the sciences. It is my contention in our thinking about disordered behaviour and people whom we currently call 'psychiatric patients'; fifty years from now when we look back on them, our current ideas will seem silly, although comprehensible in their historical context."[12] This reflects a suspicion the writer has about current empirical modes of thought. This suspicion might prove true for him when he comes to know Islam's revelation better and it comes to prevail. We have, at the moment, cases where society labels victims as schizophrenics and they suffer painfully, whereas within the context of a functioning Muslim community they could be quite healthy.

Some girls abstained from mixed, adult, sex education and the mixing of the sexes in churches etc. They were considered schizophrenic, yet this is one of the most natural, modest responses in the world from a young girl, that she feels shy of such a situation. Similarly, we have a famous case of one girl who suffered immensely when her tutors in school and then psychiatrists exerted every effort to persuade her to accept mixing with men and dating them, which they considered the social norm, and from which they saw her natural modesty and shyness as an aberration.

This is all quite contrary to the natural condition of

young girls and thus to the ethics of Islam, whose very source is naturalness, and it is contrary to the revealed law of Allah, the law that is from the same source as the very natural state aforementioned, and in harmony with it.

We could use psychological terms such as neurosis and maladjustment better in the context of a healthy Islam, where we might find that a girl who has lost that natural modesty and mixes too freely with men, is genuinely suffering from some unhealthy psychological condition and is not law abiding.

Allah, the Exalted, reveals the law in this context, and we must underline that it is the human's predicament to fall out of line with his own nature and to need revelation to remind him of what, for the animal kingdom would be its spontaneous natural state. Allah says, "And say to the believing women that they cast down their eyes and guard their private parts and reveal not their adornment save such as is outward[13]. And let them cast their veils over their bosoms, and not reveal their adornments save to their husbands, or their fathers, or their husbands' fathers, or their sons, or their husbands' sons, or their brothers, or their brothers' sons, or their sisters' sons, or their women or the slaves whom their right hands possess, or such male servants who attend them not having sexual desire, or children who have not yet attained knowledge of women's private parts, and that they should not stamp their feet in order to draw attention to their hidden ornaments. **And turn together in repentance to Allah, O believers, so that you might find success.**"

(Qur'an 24: 31).

The law is very clear in outlining the behaviour of men and women and the different orbits and circuits that they move within, in order to safeguard them, and particularly the susceptible hearts of women, to keep them pure for the worship of Allah. The law secures and guards the husband-wife relationship which is so easily damaged in today's world. Women's hearts are sensitive. In many cases an unhappy marriage leads to a miserable life. Protecting the family leads to the protection of society, the land and the Muslims. Women are vital in the transmission of society's knowledge to the next generation and in the up-bringing of children generally. Keeping the family chaste will lead to the cleanliness of society and country, or the body of Muslims in general. Once this base is corrupt everything goes wrong, then look to the destruction of society.

If you have a careful look at the *ayah* (31), you will feel the importance of it in our lives. Even children should not enter women's quarters, if they have become aware of women's private parts. The persons who can keep the company of women in a more intimate setting Allah clearly specifies, indeed mentions by name, e.g. sons and brothers. This shows how important it is to describe clearly and unambiguously the two orbits of men and women within the society, and that they don't unrestrainedly spill across each other. Allah creates us, and He knows well about His creation, indeed better than we, the creation, know about ourselves. He knows the best behaviour for them so that they can have a life blessed by Him. Trust and security lie in the submission to Allah that is, unavoidably, a radical change from inherited, habitual behaviour. Obedience to Allah needs strong determination.

The current norm when considering such illnesses as schizophrenia is quite different from how Muslims have viewed them within the context of a fully functioning, healthy Islamic society. At present if a girl or boy abstains from dating, mixing with members of the opposite sex, or promiscuity, then their society considers them abnormal. There are some cases where society labelled its victims as schizophrenics and they have suffered much pain in consequence. All the efforts of the psychiatric profession are only to return them to the social norm whether that norm is natural, sane in itself, ethical, or in accord with divine law. The psychiatrist himself has been brought up within the existing set up, he is quite unable to see beyond it, and so to him it appears normal. He himself can only change by seeing how much he is a product of that set up and by attaining a true knowledge of Allah who is beyond every social nexus. Until then the psychiatrist is only a policeman for that society's norms, no matter how perverted those norms are. Indeed it is quite sad and tragic that most people, even the highly educated such as psychiatrists, live in ignorance of the natural and harmonious way that is the truth of Islam. Until they come to such knowledge it is inevitable that most psychiatric treatment will look at the clinical picture upside-down when compared to Islamic ethics, especially in the treatment of schizophrenia.

The current treatment of split personality is to return the patient to the current norm of behaviour, regardless of whether that behaviour departs from all standards of ethics. Indeed, one who is deprived of knowledge of ethics cannot transmit it. The yardstick for treatment should be scientific, Islamic, psychonomic behaviour, based on the revealed truths of the Qur'an. It is painful for us to know that most psychopathic patients under treatment, after release remain locked in a condition of permanent insanity and anguish which the therapy has only managed to paper over but not cure. The treatment is a pseudo one. Why is that?

Some patients suffer from a very clear condition, polytheism, which even a superficial reading of Qur'an could identify. This is due to wrong up-bringing, in both knowledge of the nature of the reality of their Creator and right conduct. The most serious matter in existence is to imagine that the Divine needs partners to manage existence. Thus it is abhorrent to the intellect to claim divinity for a prophet, or that he is a son of god, or one of a trinity, or to claim any form of incarnation for the Divinity; Allah is far from what such people ascribe.

I will try to show in this book that Allah is Great and Vast beyond all imagination, that He is High and Exalted above the condition that such people assert. I will try to clarify this, in what I have called a "Theory of Relativity" to draw attention to the insignificance of the human being. He is insignificant compared to the universe, eternity, and his Creator. I mean to put the human being in the right perspective as only a SLAVE of Allah, with one mission upon earth: to worship and serve Allah without taking anything else as a partner to Allah. If one examines honestly one would have to admit that such deviations are the major reasons for almost all pernicious psychopathic illnesses, schizophrenia, dementia, neuroses, hallucinations and anxiety, etc.

Belief in multiple powers governing the world or none at all, places one under the curse and the wrath of Allah. By that curse one becomes aberrant and commits perverted deeds. Some are crippled by agonies of conscience because people regard them as suffering from pathological states. The power of Allah shakes the very earth under their feet. Having become manic they run to the haven provided, as they think, by the psychiatrists, who can do no more for them than sedate them and try to bring them back to what is merely a social norm. Some such carry seeds of great crimes, in their hearts, which they conceal from society by assuming masks and identities in front of people. Psychiatrists try to neutralise the very real guilt these aberrants feel about their criminal conditions and present their criminal tendencies to them as normal. They live in society as latent criminals. Other therapists try to develop in them social skills so that these poor deviants' criminal acts are screened or masked by their social activities. This is merely a continuation of the old church system of the priest hearing confession and then granting forgiveness to the sinner who felt temporarily relieved as if by a sedative but then went out to sin again. No-one can grant forgiveness but Allah, to whom one turns in repentance from one's wrong actions. It is imperative that one then carries on in an upright manner rather than becoming locked into the vicious cycle of wrong action, repentance and forgiveness and then wrong action again.

Clearly psychiatrists, by and large, have adopted the

mantle of the priest. There is no cure for the root disease, no treatment for the original cause, so they offer sedation or a route back to the social norm. Even where there is a neurological cure for a neuroma (tumour), by a means such as surgery, it is clear that as long as the main cause has not been addressed the patient must after some time return to the original situation. The societal picture that emerges is corruption at every level. Maintaining an aberrant society as it is, only leads to widespread moral pollution and disintegration. Such a society can only meet the devastating consequences of its own actions here and in the next life.

Allah, the Exalted says, "Our command comes upon it by night or by day, and We make it like a harvest which is clean-mown, as though yesterday it did not flourish."

(Qur'an 10: 24).

Again Allah, the Exalted, says, "Do the people of the cities feel secure that Our might shall not come upon them at night while they are sleeping? Do the people of the cities feel secure that Our might shall not come upon them in broad daylight while they are playing? Do they feel secure against the devising of Allah? None feel secure against the devising of Allah except those doomed to ruin."

(Qur'an 7: 97).

The words of Allah never fail. The close of the twentieth century has witnessed the fall of communism. The world will, until the end of time, witness the shattering into pieces of every philosophy which is astray from the path of Allah. Now that communism has been exposed for what it is many other false philosophies will similarly be exposed as the obstacles they are to real knowledge of Allah, and to belief and trust in Him. So any ideology or creed, other than the religion of Islam, is utter loss. Any attitude other than Islam (submission) is total loss.

Most people are in real need of a path to the purification of the self, and to acquiring a genuine feeling of inner, along with outer, security. These they can begin to obtain through the qualities of uprightness and sincere turning from wrong action to Allah. One has to abide by His prohibitions and His commandments and then turn sincerely and genuinely to Him in full submission, i.e. in Islam.

Islam is the most exact of all sciences. One may study and learn it as a subject but then one must embody it in order to arrive at its fruits; the knowledge of security and safety. If one took as much care to learn about Islam as one devotes to other lesser subjects one would then be able to embark on the discovery of one's true nature and selfhood and become a healthy human being. The alternative is the path of anxiety, frustration and insanity.

One who wanted to specialise in any technical field, e.g. computers, would exert every effort to master the knowledge necessary. So it is with Islam, which contains the most exact and definite statement on the nature of reality.

Peoples and nations have failed to establish just Islamic governance due to their deviation from the correct application of the *shariah* law of Islam. That is because of their bending the laws of Allah to their own purposes according to their whims. The questions of monotheism (*tawhid*) and of the nature and status of women are two of the major issues facing mankind, let alone the Muslims. Some have favoured emancipation of women and others tried to evade the command in the *ayah* we considered earlier (Qur'an 24: 31) in order to please a sector of the people, on the face of it, but actually only following hidden lust and caprice. Yet what is pleasure? Is it a pleasure to guide someone to the Fire through wrong up-bringing?

Islam is pure submission to Allah. Trying to find ways around Allah's instructions rather than simply abiding by them is to go astray. To whom then is one submitting? Allah, the Blessed and Exalted, says, "Allah does not forgive that anything should be associated with Him (as a partner). And He forgives less than that to whomever He wills. Whoever associates anything with Allah has gone far astray. They pray not, apart from Him, except to female beings and they pray not, apart from Him, except to a rebellious Shaytan."

(Qur'an 4: 116-117).

If one multiplies 2×2, the result is 4. It can never be 3 or 5. If one wants to find the area of a rectangle then one multiplies the length by the breadth. But if one multiplies the breadth by the breadth one will not find the area of that rectangle but of a square. In the laboratory, oxygen and hydrogen mixed in the ratio of one molecule of the former to every two of the latter yields water, H_2O. If the ratio is not adhered to the result will be something else.

Islam is just such an exact science. To achieve full Islamic governance, under which Allah is worshipped and obeyed sincerely and purely, one has to ensure that the *ayats* of the Qur'an and the Sunnah of His Prophet, *salla'llahu alaihi wa sallam,* are applied, and that one's submission is to Allah alone. The Muslim always watches his relationship with his Lord. Is it on a monotheistic, a dualistic or polytheistic basis? This inward relationship is confirmed in the outward by the manner in which the Muslim enacts the law of Allah.

Allah states in Qur'an, about the expulsion of humanity from the Garden: "We said, 'Get you down, all of you from it (the Garden). And if, as is sure, there comes to you from Me a guidance, then whoever follows My guidance, there shall be no fear upon them neither shall they grieve. And the ones who disbelieve and deny Our *ayats,* then those are the companions of the Fire, they abide therein.'"
(Qur'an 2: 38-39).

The society without law, which does not bind itself by the natural law of Allah, will always be in unrest, turmoil and in endless trouble and mutual enmity. That is true whether the society is a group, a party, a community, or a country.

In a small pamphlet entitled *The Third Wave and Education Futures,* William C. Miller wrote:

"All around us is evidence that things aren't working, and there is a vague but growing concern about the direction in which our society seems to be drifting.

"We view with alarm the crime, inflation, hedonistic behaviour and shifts of values around us. In addition, we see an increasing frequency of personality disorders, and mental illness. There seems to be a loss of inner harmony and a decreased sense of purpose. Many have noted a disheartening decline in their sense of community. People do not feel 'connected' and are concerned about their growing sense of depersonalisation. All about is a pervasive sense of despair. Individuals feel lost, powerless and hopeless. The vision of the years is bleak, and we seem not to be able to agree on which direction to take for the common good. It is as if America were having a nervous breakdown."

In most parts of the world, in Europe, in England, in Africa or the Far East, etc. this is the state of affairs. Everywhere there is an education directed merely to existing and surviving then to hedonism, rather than to the building of human beings with profound moral character, ethics and awe of the Creator. In this case how can there be a sound, healthy society?

I hope now that the picture is clear and complete. One may not despair however bad the situation. Regeneration can be achieved by a will and determination to travel on the path to Allah, the Exalted. One starts with one step in order to set out for the Garden of Bliss.

THE ARABIC LANGUAGE
Must Be Learnt World-wide

Many read translations of the Qur'an in their own languages, but unfortunately they receive a distorted view of the revelation. This is primarily due to a lack of knowledge of the Arabic language, from which knowledge emerges the sweetness, vigour, truth, clarity, coherence and wisdom of the Qur'an. There are a great number of mistaken translations in some of the English versions which deprive the reader of the proper meaning. For example, "The prophet of the common folk" is more correctly translated as "The prophet who can neither read nor write" since it is important to indicate the unlettered and untutored nature of the Prophet, *salla'llahu alaihi wa sallam*, because it shows the great miracle that is the Qur'an and that is the revelation of the way of Islam. "I swear by the falling stars" ought to read "I swear by the positions of the stars" because it refers to the positions of the stars in the heavens, held in their mathematical orbits by the Designer, the All-Knowing Creator. These translations miss the right meanings and even where the meaning is technically correct they miss out the vital scent of the words of Qur'an. It is like robbing the rainbow of its ravishing, iridescent, multifarious colours or the honey of its sweetness.

People must exert then, every effort to learn the Arabic language, just as many of us have spent years of our lives, learning, reading and studying the English language, until we were able to understand it well and express ourselves clearly. I hope, *insha'Allah*, to convey, with my modest knowledge of English, these few thoughts to other English speakers all over the world, for the sake of Allah alone, and in order to transmit His revelation and the Sunnah of the Seal of the Prophets, Muhammad, *salla'llahu alaihi wa sallam*. I ask Allah that He make the teaching of Islam and of the Arabic language universal in the educational institutions of the world, as a key to, and a means of safety on, the right path of Allah, the path which leads to the garden of bliss. (See Qur'an 3: 85).

When we look at the efforts exerted in this life, and how some people wear themselves out for the sake of this temporal and temporary existence, one would imagine that many think they are going on a sort of vacation after their deaths from which they will return to live forever in this world.

We must call people to wake up and return to Allah. Muslims must return to Allah, their root and origin, and be helpful to the uninformed without bitterness, to teach them Islam in all its majesty and simplicity.

Racial discrimination, ethnic divisions, and all social problems are solved by a true knowledge of Allah under the banner of Islam.

Allah, the Blessed and Exalted, says, "O mankind, We have created you from male and female and We have made you peoples and tribes that you may know one another. The noblest of you in the sight of Allah is the best of you in conduct. Truly, Allah is all-knowing, all-aware."

(Qur'an 49: 13).

Life is transient. Good deeds wipe out the bad. Trust and faith are the vital issues. Allah, the Glorious and Exalted, says, "Truly, in the creation of the heavens and the earth, and in the alternation of night and day, there are signs for people of understanding, the ones who remember Allah standing, sitting and upon their sides, and who reflect upon the creation of the heavens and the earth, 'Our Lord, You have not created this in vain, glory be to You. Save us from the anguish of the fire.'"

(Qur'an 3: 190-191).

Praise and thanks be to Allah who has guided us to this. As the angels said to their Creator in the Qur'an, "We have no knowledge save that which You have taught us. Truly it is You who are the All-Knowing, the All-Wise." (Qur'an 2: 32).

The Seed and the Sperm

"Our Lord, condemn us not, if we forget or we make a mistake; Our Lord, lay not on us a burden like that which You laid upon those before us; Our Lord, do not lay upon us a burden greater than we have the strength to bear; and pardon us, and forgive us and have mercy on us. You are our Master, so help us against the ones who disbelieve."

(Qur'an 2: 286).

All praise belongs to Allah, the Almighty, for making me one of the Muslims following the teachings of the Prophet Muhammad, *salla'llahu alaihi wa sallam*, and of Ibrahim, *alaihi's-salaam*.

Muhammad Abbas Nadeem
Al Madinah Al Munawwarah,
1/8/1414 H (Jan. – 1994)

CHAPTER ONE

The Necessity of Contemplation

Allah, the Blessed and Exalted, frequently affirms the necessity of contemplation in the Qur'an.

"Truly, in the creation of the heavens and the earth, and in the alternation of night and day, there are signs for people of understanding, the ones who remember Allah standing, sitting and upon their sides, and who reflect upon the creation of the heavens and the earth, 'Our Lord, You have not created this in vain, glory be to You. Save us from the anguish of the fire.'"

(Qur'an 3: 190-191).

Contemplation leads to conviction. As we saw, the Prophet Ibrahim, *alaihi's-salaam*, arrived at certainty through contemplation of the heavens and the earth. He reflected upon the creation, the stars, the moon and the sun, and then he said, "Truly I have set my face towards the One who created the heavens and the earth, as one by nature inclining to the truth, and I am not one of those who ascribe partners to Allah." This same path can be taken by any human being whether he is a scientist, a geographer, a biologist, etc., or not, to reach a knowledge which is convincing, the point of clear faith and certitude. Let us explore together the following *ayats* of Allah in His Qur'an, as an effort in contemplation of the creation of Allah.

The Seed and the Sperm

"And We have made the heaven a well-protected canopy; yet they turn away from Our signs." (Qur'an 21: 32). The *ayah* describes the atmosphere, the azure spherical dome (the near sky above us), reaching to about two hundred kilometres above the earth. It is a beauty beyond imagination especially at that spot where the great mosque lies, the *Ka'abah*, the sacred House of Allah, which every Muslim faces for his prayer. It starts black like a scholar's gown and one feels the depth and serenity of the night, then it gradually changes with the early gentle breath of the morning into a deep azure blue. Then it slowly fades away into a faint purple, then to white until it becomes as white as fluffy spun cotton. The sky, in its deep blueness, seems so near that one could almost touch it with one's fingers. One could hardly witness such a spectacular scene anywhere in the whole world. It is one of the most remarkably beautiful pictures, the like of which I had never seen in my life previously. This, the nearer part of the sky that one sees above one, is a ceiling designed to act as a shield to the land against falling meteors and meteorites, which occasionally burst into multitudes of particles on impact. Nitrogen gas, which is in abundance, works as a fire-extinguisher. It is very rare for the earth to be hit by a falling meteor, for the atmosphere to let one through, except when Allah permits it to happen as a punishment upon some people, or sends it down as a warning. Sometimes unjust and corrupt peoples have been rained upon by piercing stones from the sky. This is not just an occurrence of the ancient times, indeed it may still happen to peoples in the future, as Allah stated in the Qur'an.

The Necessity of Contemplation

Allah, the Exalted says, "When Our decree came, We turned them (the cities) upside down and rained on them stones hard as black clay, layer on layer, marked as from your Lord. Nor are they ever far from those who do wrong (who are unjust)."
(Qur'an 11: 83).

In the space described above, the atmosphere is kept in a marvellous balance. The oxygen desired for life is in proportion to the nitrogen, which is in abundance. The nitrogen acts as a fire extinguisher. In addition to these, there are small amounts of carbon dioxide, ozone, hydrogen etc. Each of these has its particular role in the whole structure of the universe. Plant synthesis, for example, uses carbon dioxide (CO_2) by day and the plants exhale oxygen by night. Mammals inhale oxygen and exhale carbon dioxide. The ratios of each to the other are incredibly fine and are kept by the All-Knowing to an unimaginable degree.

The bad deeds of human beings are: deviation from the right path of Allah, i.e. governance without the law of Allah, attributing partners to Allah and usury, which includes interest charged on bank investments and deposits, and corruption in every aspect of life. All of these automatically have a counter effect on the weather and the balance between the elements necessary in the atmosphere. Imbalances in heaven and earth lead to both increase and decrease in the birth rate. Sometimes for the very poor, an increase in the birth rate is a greater menace than benefit. I do not concur with the use of contraceptives. An upright life contains the best solutions for all kinds of problems. Similarly one finds decrease in the birth rates of animals and in the reproductive growth of the plant kingdom.

The aforementioned usury is a very serious matter indeed, which leads to a great curse falling on people from Allah. The income of rich people multiplies through banking mechanisms according to the rate of interest. This is an inevitable cause of global inflation, which causes rises in the prices of commodities, afflicting low income groups who are unable to benefit from interest on incomes and savings. These normally constitute the bulk of the people, who hence become poorer. Social standards of life, which demand that every house should have a refrigerator, electric lighting and running water, etc., lead lower income groups to run the risk of incurring unwise debts with banks and money-lenders. Most become victims of debtors' bad habits, which run to alcoholism, gambling and adultery. Debts are sometimes contracted between friends, although often false friends. Many contract usurious debts which exponentially grow with the interest. Grinding poverty breaks the moral fibre of families, and they try to use any means to attain their aims. The poor, it is worthwhile to note, constitute the great mass of humanity. There are many *ayats* in the Qur'an encouraging good treatment of the poor. Allah, the Exalted, made *zakah*, the tax on the wealthy for the benefit of the poor, obligatory and, furthermore, one of the essential pillars of Islam. That concern for the poor is one of the reasons that Allah forbade usury. "In order that it (wealth) may not be confined in a circuit of the wealthy among you." (Qur'an 59: 7).

What we have said about the poor can just as truthfully be said about the poor nations; their poverty leads them into debt to international usurious organisations and henceforth the curse of Allah, which is in usury, falls on them too. There is only one solution, to which there is no alternative; which is an upright life, and a genuine trust in and application of the law of Allah.

Industries have arisen in towns in abundance leading to pollution and the cancerous growth of cities, which have become great sprawling urban conurbations where civic corruption, bad behaviour and gross indecency prevail. Almost all investments in these industries have come from banking institutions. They involve loans borrowed at interest, of course, and they automatically lead to more usury by the entrepreneurs becoming active agents of usurious banks in most of their transactions. The result of this negligent and immoral behaviour, of these mini- and maxi-tycoons, is pollution of air, rivers, streams, seas and, worst of all, people, who become corrupted in every sense. Usury is one of the main factors leading to the curse of Allah. That curse spreads over every aspect of life; plant-life diseases, aridity, infestation with pests, animal and human sicknesses, neurosis, nervous breakdown, all kinds of psychopathic diseases, stunted growth of children, antagonistic, or just bad, behaviour in general, and sexual obsession, etc.

One could take as example any country where the law of Allah is not applied and where usury is practised. There are many examples. It leads to total breakdown. Education in imperialistic countries and post-colonial countries is built on capitalist theories of economics, key elements of which are monopoly, oligopoly, interest, usurious investment and banking. Universities are shrines dedicated to the inculcation of such values. This includes a political theory, which is grounded in the study of pyramidical, western thought and philosophy. As always the problem at base is very simple: the created being does not realise that he is absolutely a slave of his Creator. Therefore, because he does not realise this, he does not follow what Allah, his Benefactor and Lord, commands him to do. Instead he goes astray and follows Shaytan (Satan).

The result is as we have explained. Almost all urban development problems arise from, breakdown in conduct, polytheism (i.e. seeing existence as dominated by a multiplicity of powers rather than the One power) deviation from the path to Allah and usury. There are now some sincere efforts to establish the true Islamic economy in accordance with the *shariah* of Allah, which one hopes will become universal.

The Qur'an is very clear on Allah's prohibition of usury:

"Allah deprives usury of blessing but He gives increase (lit: interest) for acts of charity. And Allah does not love every guilty ungrateful one."

(Qur'an 2: 276).

"O you who believe, fear Allah and abandon what remains of usury if you are believers. Then, if you don't, take notice of war from Allah and His Messenger. If you turn (from your wrong action) then you have the principal of your properties, not wronging nor being wronged."

(Qur'an 2: 278-279).

Allah, the Sublime and Exalted, made and measured out all provision of sustenance in four days:

The Necessity of Contemplation

"Say, 'Is it that you deny Him who created the earth in two days and do you set up equals with Him? That is the Lord of the worlds. He set on it (the earth) mountains standing firm on top of it and bestowed blessing on it, and decreed in it its nourishment in four days, alike for those who ask."

(Qur'an 41: 9-10).

That nourishment is not an easy thing to imagine. It included the volume of water needed for all mankind, the animals, the birds, etc., from the beginning of the creation of the earth to its end. It included vegetation of every kind, trees that grow fruits of different tastes and colours, and crops and cereals of all sorts of sizes and manifold uses. It included the animals, both domesticated and wild, the birds, the fish, etc., those that are for consumption, by man and other creatures, and those that are to live free and untamed, or tamed, to multiply. Had he submitted in obedience to his Creator, man would have lived in peace and contentment. Shortages and economic waste are mainly due to falling foul of the Creator's justice. The giving and taking of usury lead to the corruption of the beautiful and bountiful creation of Allah. In turn this disobedience leads to the vengeance of Allah through volcanoes, desertification, floods, all kinds of pests, plagues of locusts and wars. Allah and His Messenger wage war on those who practice usury. Allah also punishes those who break His divinely revealed laws. The last of the shariahs is contained in the Qur'an, but it is unfortunate that for many the Qur'an has become merely something to sing heedlessly. So people meet shortages, recessions and inflation, due to their own bad deeds and their disobedience of the law of Allah (See Qur'an 42: 30, 30: 41-42). Otherwise they would have lived in peace, prosperity and contentment until the Last Day (See Qur'an 5: 65-66).

"O you who believe, fear Allah and give up what remains of usury if you are believers. And if you do not then take notice of a war from Allah and His Messenger. And if you turn (from your wrong action) then you will have the principal sums of your capital, neither wronging nor being wronged."

(Qur'an 2: 278-279).

These astonishing *ayats* are the yardstick with which to measure the origins of almost all wars which have taken place recently or in the past. They are supported by other *ayats* of Qur'an which reflect the consequence of illicit, or downright evil, gain. Wrongly acquired earnings lead to corruption, whether it is physical, spiritual or even, pollution from industrial development.

"Mischief (corruption) has appeared on land and sea, because of that which the hands of people have earned, that Allah may give them a taste of some of their deeds, that they might return (from their wrong actions)."

(Qur'an 30: 41).

"Whatever misfortune happens to you is because of the things your hands have gained, and He pardons much."

(Qur'an 42: 30).

"They are fond of listening to falsehood, often devouring the forbidden ...". (Qur'an 5: 42).

Allah gives examples of such nations which He has subjected to grievous punishment:

"As for Thamoud We gave them guidance, but they preferred blindness to guidance so the stunning punishment of humiliation seized them because of what they used to earn."
(Qur'an 41: 17).

This issue of usury is of course related to the major matters, which are that rulers do not apply the revealed law of Allah, and that people follow their appetites and their caprices. The reasons given for wars and catastrophes are always superficial. They hide the fact that people have, one way or another, deviated from the right path. Going astray leads to imbalance whether in the atmosphere, the oceans or the land. Misuse and excessive use of chlorofluore compounds (e.g. methane) in refrigeration, air-conditioning, some aviation and some sprays, have had a drastic effect upon the ozone layer which acts as a protection against the excessive heat of the sun and keeps a reasonable temperature in the environment. This natural planetary ceiling is designed with certain ratios of gases to protect us from the harmful radiation of sun beams, allowing through only that which is useful to life. Everything is held in its unique ratio of optimum benefit, and misuse leads to perilous imbalances.

Contemplation is the essence of worship. One way to achieve it is to read the Qur'an reflectively, trying to understand it, and by looking for the truth and the perfect order in the universe indicated by *ayats* of the Qur'an. With an observant eye and an intelligent heart one can discern clearly the omnipotence of the Creator shown by the movements of the planets, stars, sun and moon, and in how the movements of the earth in relation to the sun bring about the majestic splendour of the sunset, which is the withdrawal of daylight from night, like stripping the skin from a sheep, as Allah, the Exalted describes it:

"And a sign for them is the night, We withdraw the day from it and, behold, they are plunged in darkness."
(Qur'an 36: 37).
And how beautifully the astronomical bodies swim in the cosmos:

"It is not permitted to the sun to catch up the moon, nor can the night outstrip the day. Each is in an orbit swimming."
(Qur'an 36: 40).

It is all a work of art, so beautiful is it beyond imagining, so captivating with its spell of beauty, order and heavenly majesty. There is nothing haphazard, no place for chance. It is from the All-Wise, the All-Knowing, the All-Powerful, the Vast Creator. How wonderful their orbiting! The same applies to all the planets, asteroids and other satellites, all of them glorify the Creator, but we don't understand their glorification. The thunder, so thrilling and breath-taking, the stars, the mountains, the birds, the bees and all the vegetation, everything in the universe glorifies Allah, the Vast and prostrates to Him.

"Whatever is in the heavens and the earth glorifies Allah. To Him belongs the kingdom, and to Him belongs the praise. And He is able to do all things."
(Qur'an 64: 1).

"The seven heavens and the earth and all beings therein declare His glory. There is not a thing but that it glorifies with praise of Him. However, you do not

understand their glorification. Truly, He is Oft-Forbearing, Most Forgiving."
(Qur'an 17: 44).

"The thunder glorifies with praise of Him, and the angels from awe of Him."
(Qur'an 13: 13).

"And We compelled the mountains, along with Dawud, to glorify, and the birds."
(Qur'an 21: 79).

"The sun and the moon follow courses (exactly) computed. And the star and the trees prostrate."
(Qur'an 55: 5-6).

Everything works according to His vast will producing the most defined order. Allah has revealed a superb description of His creation in the Qur'an. The Prophet, *salla'llahu alaihi wa sallam*, also describes the creation in an extraordinary manner, descriptions which are recorded in the *hadith* literature. Minute details of the processes are given to those whom Allah blesses with knowledge. The same applies to those whom Allah permits the knowledge of astronomy, mathematics and geography, etc. Knowledge is given by the All-Knowing. Qur'an contains very general statements the details of which are permitted to those whom Allah blesses with knowledge:

"He is the one who made the sun to shine and the moon to be a light and measured it (the moon) in phases in order that you might know the number of the years and the reckoning. Allah did not create that but with the truth. We detail the signs for a people who know."
(Qur'an 10: 5).

The Seed and the Sperm

Allah describes the sun and the moon swimming in the cosmos. He describes how the moon appears in phases until it wanes and becomes similar to the old stalk of a palm tree's leaf. Look at the wonderful order of the moon, the sun and our earth. Everything is measured and precise to the decimal point.

"And the moon We have measured in phases until it returns like the old (withered) lower part of a date stalk." (Qur'an 36: 39).

By this it was intended for us to know the numbers of the years and the reckoning. This includes all sciences of mathematics, astronomy and space sciences.

Allah swears by the accuracy of the positions of the stars (i.e. celestial objects; galaxies, novae, super-novae, planets and other satellites):

"I swear by the positions of the stars and truly it is an oath, which if only you knew is vast, truly it is a noble Qur'an in a well-guarded book."

(Qur'an 56: 75-78).

Some of the stars, planets and galaxies have taken centuries to be discovered and their positions known accurately. The discoveries of the means for astronomical investigation and space exploration, starting from the telescope and including space-ships and satellites, have taken a very long time. We have only begun on this path. This age may be characterised as the age of information explosion. It has had some good results, in that some have realised the Presence of the Creator, and have submitted to Allah by embracing Islam. There are those who have written valuable works, using their scientific training, to expound a true knowledge of, and belief in, Allah and the last of His prophets, Muhammad, *salla'llahu alaihi wa sallam,* and the glorious Qur'an revealed to him through the angel Jibril (Gabriel). These are advances indeed, but it should be our aim that this happen in every branch of knowledge. The essence of the whole matter is very simple: to come to know Allah truly and trust in Him, and to take His last revelation, the Qur'an, as a law and guidance. Yet some are so perverse that they would deny the facts. No wonder that those who disbelieve are so miserable. This extraordinary vista of the sky, its planets, galaxies and stars, the splendour and wonder of it has had a tremendous effect on people. The twentieth century, because of its literacy in the realm of space knowledge, shuns the corrupted relics of ancient mythologies. To the decadent later generations of the ancients some of the stellar and planetary motions seemed to reflect the caprices of super beings. The old Greek and Roman legends are well known. Mars was the god of war, Venus the goddess of love. Very few people see it like that now. Man-made vehicles now circle Mars and Venus and land on them. These massive planetary globes of stone, gas, iron and other elements, have genuine material significance, rather than mythological meaning, in our lives[1].

You can see how scientific understanding and technological prowess has effaced older mythological visions, particularly those debased and idolatrous ones we have referred to.

Shakespeare, reflecting as he did the age he lived in, evinces a great deal of such spurious beliefs. Some of his plays treat of Greek and Roman mythology. You find the salient trait of swearing by the planets, or the

The Seed and the Sperm

mythological figures of the same names, Jupiter and Mars. Some of the characters take the heavenly bodies as good and bad omens, and signs of the fates of emperors. Worse than that is the taking of celestial objects as deities. For example:

Ulysses. If thou wouldst not entomb thyself
alive,
  And case thy reputation in thy tent;
  Whose glorious deeds, but in these fields of
late,
  Made emulous missions 'mongst the gods
themselves,
  And drave great Mars to faction.
  (Troilus and Cressida).

Aufidius.   O Marcius, Marcius!
Each word thou hast spoken hath weeded
from my heart
  a root of ancient envy. If Jupiter
  should from yond' cloud speak divine things,
  and say 'Tis true', I'd not believe them more.
  (Coriolanus).

Marcus Andronicus. Sit down, sweet niece;
brother, sit down by me.
  Apollo, Pallas, Jove, or Mercury,
  Inspire me, that I may this treason find.
  (Titus Andronicus).
  Lear. By Jupiter, I swear, no.
  Kent. By Juno, I swear, ay.
  (King Lear).

The Necessity of Contemplation

To keep our monotheistic knowledge of the Divinity alive it is vital to read the Qur'an, which has been kept intact by the will of Allah, and understand the nature of existence and the Divine, from the original source reference work. Contemplation is a method which has been urged by the prophets since Nuh, *alaihi's-salaam*.

"What is the matter with you that you are not conscious of Allah's majesty, seeing that He has created you in stages? Do you not consider how Allah has created seven heavens in layers and He has made the moon in them as a light and He made the sun a radiant lamp (in the sense of giving light and warmth)?"

(Qur'an, Surah Nuh: 13-16).

The Qur'an is replete with invitations to reflection, that the believer might move on to the condition of conviction and certainty. Certainty must be the ultimate aim of people, particularly those who have the extra responsibility of governing the affairs of people. That is because someone having deep conviction and faith in Allah will not be shaken while making decisions, regardless of public support, opposition or opinion, as long as he is fully aware that he is carrying out the law of Allah and obeying His commands. The same is true of the learned. Certainty, generally, gives peace of mind, clarity of thought, and wisdom.

Allah repeatedly calls on us to reflect. How extraordinary! For you can never reach satiety of reflection!

"Do they not consider the camels and how they were created, the heaven and how it was raised up, the mountains and how they were erected, and the earth and how it was stretched out?"

(Qur'an 88: 17-20).

The Seed and the Sperm

Mountains are like the pegs which keep the earth from being convulsed.

"Did we not make the earth an expanse and the mountains bulwarks?"

(Qur'an 78: 6-7).

As you can see, normally the Qur'an makes general statements and then scientists, geologists, geographers, etc., find out the details, the knowledge of which sometimes takes them centuries to reach. Faith leads to proper guidance, in a short time, by the will of Allah. The mountains reach down into the crust of the earth, the upper layer of which is about five kilometres thick. At the points where the mountains lie, the thickness is about thirty kilometres. The mountains are exactly like bulwarks; they are very steadfast in the sima layer.

"He created the heavens without pillars you can see, and He cast on the earth firm mountains lest it shake with you. He scattered on the earth every kind of creature, and We sent down from the sky water, and caused to grow in it (the earth) every noble pair. This is the creation of Allah, so show me what those apart from Him created. Rather, wrongdoers are in clear error."

(Qur'an 31: 10-11).

"And He cast into the earth firm mountains lest it should quake with you and rivers and roads that you might be guided."

(Qur'an 16: 15).

It is quite obvious that Allah, the Creator, is the One who gives sustenance to all living creatures on earth, in the rivers, at the bottom of the sea, as well as to the species of the plant kingdom of every kind and hue.

All praise is due to Him, the Almighty

CHAPTER TWO

The Seed and the Sperm

The Qur'an and the Sunnah are our terms of reference and the main basis for the exploration of our topic, *The Seed and the Sperm* these two prominent elements of the creational process. Allah, the Exalted, has created the seed and the sperm and nobody is allowed to create the like of them, or more truly no-one is able to do so. From these two come all plant and animal life. From these two Allah gave health, wealth and activity. Water is the material of which they are primarily composed. "And from water We made every living thing."

(Qur'an 21: 30).

"We created you. So what if you do not affirm? Have you considered that which you ejaculate, is it you who create it or are We the creators? We have decreed among you death and We shall not be outstripped from exchanging the likes of you and creating you anew in that which you do not know."

(Qur'an 56: 57-61).

"Have you considered that which you cultivate, is it you who cause it to grow or are We the causes?"

(Qur'an 56: 63-64).

"Have you considered the water which you drink, did you send it down from the rain clouds or are We the senders down?" (Qur'an 56: 68-69).

The Seed and the Sperm

Abu Hurayra narrated, *radiya'llahu 'anhu* (may Allah be pleased with him), that the Messenger of Allah, *salla'llahu alaihi wa sallam*, said, "Allah said, 'Who is more wrongdoing that he who tries to create the like of My creation. Let them create a tiny insect. Let them create a seed or a barleycorn.'"[1]

"O mankind, remember the blessing of Allah upon you. Is there a creator other than Allah who gives you sustenance from the heaven and the earth. There is no god but Him. So how then are you deluded?"

(Qur'an 35: 3).

"And a sign for them is the dead earth, We make it live and We produce from out of it grain so that from it they eat. And We make in it gardens of date-palms and of vines and We cause springs to gush forth in them that they might eat of its fruits and from what their hands make[2]. Will they not then give thanks[3]? Glory be to Allah who created the pairs, all of them, from that which the earth grows and from themselves and from that which they do not know."

(Qur'an 36: 34-36).

"Let man consider his food. We poured the rains abundantly, then We split the earth in fissures, and We made to grow in it grains and vines and reeds and olives and date-palms, and gardens densely tree-filled, and fruits, and pasture, as an enjoyment for you and for your flocks."

(Qur'an 80: 24-32).

THE SEED

A general scientific description, stated by Professor Hynes, is as follows:

"Almost all seeds possess three types of structure, a covering (seed coat or testa), and a young sporophyte (the embryo) and a food supply (female gameto phytic tissue, endosperm and/or cotyledons). Indeed, a seed has been poetically described as 'a baby plant in a box with its lunch'.

"The seed coat may be soft or hard, thick or thin, permeable or impermeable to water, dry or fleshy. The seed coat does function, however, as a protection to the structures that it contains. The part of the seed that continues to grow upon germination is the embryo. The embryo results from the zygote that is produced when the egg is fertilised. Therefore, the zygote is the beginning of the next sporophyte generation.

"The food supply is the source of energy for the start and continuation of growth of the young sporophyte until it can become photosynthetic and begin producing its own food."[4]

The scientific description, quoted above, shows the marvellous creation of Allah and its splendour. Yet the seed is a known element of creation in the plant kingdom. The cycle of plant creation is: the seed, the plant, the flower, pollination, the fruit and again a seed, ... etc. It is a fascinating cycle.

The original Maker and Organiser of all these processes of development is Allah, the One, the All-Mighty. It is His mighty will to say to a thing 'Be' and it 'Is'. Isa, *alaihi's-salaam*, was born through this command. Allah has referred to this command in the Qur'an:

"His command, when He desires a thing, is only that He says to it 'Be' and it 'Is'. So glory be to Him in whose hand is the kingship of every thing and to whom you

The Seed and the Sperm

will be returned."

(Qur'an 36: 82-83).

It is really fascinating to contemplate the cycle of generation of the plant, to see the power of Allah in the creation. The cycle starts sometimes within the flower which bears the male and female gametes and by their fusion together, like that of the sperm and the ovum, emerges the fruit and within it the seed.

Sometimes the cycle of development happens through the transfer of pollen grains from the flower of one plant by a butterfly, an ant or a human being, carried without the knowledge of the carrier to another flower, thus causing pollination.

Sometimes the wind pollinates, driving male pollen to the female which happens to lie in the course of the wind. For some plants, like the date-palm, pollination can happen through the agency of the wind, or by the intentional action of someone transferring male pollen grains to the female. From that the dates come. It is all the sublime organisation of the supreme Organiser. The fruit in most cases carries the seed.

The Creator is One, and a person can trace and follow this Oneness through the creation. The original idea of male and female is characteristic of this Oneness of source. The process of fertilisation, zygote, embryo, tree, flower, fruit and then seed again, is identical to the steps in the animal, bird and human kingdoms. It tells of one governing mode of creation, and that the Creator is One.

"And of all the fruits He makes on it (the earth) two of a pair."

(Qur'an 13: 3).

"We caused to grow in it (the earth) every noble pair (of plants)."

(Qur'an 31: 10).

"You see the ground lifeless, then when We send upon it the water it shakes and grows, and puts forth every magnificent pair of plants."

(Qur'an 22: 5).

It is clear that knowledge is deeper than the face value of things. There is a relation between material existence and the unseen. Knowledge reflects the unseen greatness behind creation. It thus becomes contemplation of creation, a higher state of mind, and a worship by all the senses. This is what makes the difference between a machine, such as a photocopier which reproduces images, or a manufacturing machine which produces spare-parts, and a human being with a living heart and feelings, whose senses and mind are alert and who develops in wisdom by his recognition of the Creator. This is the message of education and the profit from knowledge; it is related in all respects to the Creator. It is not a question of learning bare facts without any pause to understand their origin. It is not about memorising data as in most botany references, without a pause to consider Him Who created. Knowledge without faith is pointless, aimless and in the end rather vague.

DISTINCT CREATION

None of mankind, whether male, female, king, commoner, genius, powerful or wealthy, can ever create a seed. They can, by the will of Allah, crossbreed or transplant but never create a seed. For who from mankind has ever done so since the beginning of creation? And who can, from now till the Last Day? No-one can create any seed from which the plant grows upon this earth, angiosperm or gymnosperm of any type from among all the varieties of fruits, vegetables, cereals, and trees. It is the distinct creation of Allah and a unique sign of His will and His Presence everywhere. This creation of the seed is His, genuinely and uniquely, totally His property. When we understand that we must know also that all creation is as totally His, of His making. Even the human acts of cross-breeding plants, are from His absolute will. All knowledge is from Him and all is His. Nobody can gain His knowledge except by His will and with His consent. If one keeps a secret or hides it from another, no-one can know it except if one tells it to them. Similarly, for Allah the Highest, no-one can gain His knowledge from Him except by His will.

Despite technological breakthroughs, space-ships and moon-landings, mankind still has very meagre knowledge, as Allah declares in Qur'an: "And you have not been given of knowledge but a little."

(Qur'an 17: 85).

Allah has allowed us to reach the moon and the planets, and to master genetic engineering and it is by His will: "We will show them Our signs on the horizons and in themselves till it is clear to them that He is the truth. Does it not suffice as to your Lord that He is able to do all things?"

(Qur'an 41: 53).

Allah is He who creates the mind, the senses, all the faculties, the plants, the planets, the sun, the moon, the heavens and the earth and everything between the two of them. He is the sole Owner, as we have seen and will see in this book, of the origin of all beings. It is His creation alone, and He is the All-Powerful over it, the One and only God who has no equal, the Creator of all that exists.

THE UTILITY OF THE SEED

If we look at the seed and what grows from it, as one example of the creation, we shall see clearly the gifts of Allah to us, the bread we eat, the tables we use, the beds we sleep upon, the cloth with which we clothe ourselves, the sweet juices we drink, the sweetly fragrant flowers we smell, the green grass upon which the family reposes in tranquillity and joy on a beautiful sunny day, house-doors which are plainly and solidly made or beautifully decorated, houses of timber construction for habitation or shelter, or as sheds for domestic animals and birds; all these and much more spring ultimately from the seed and its produce.

Allah creates the seed. It is of different uses to mankind as well as to the birds and the animals, but I will focus on its utility to the human being. Suppose that x purchased timber from y, shaped it into chairs, blackboards, cupboards and tables, and then sold it at a profit to z (a number of other people). This means that there is a material gain. Money has been earned by which one purchases other things and so the monetary cycle. Remember though that the origin is that which issued from a seed, in this example, timber. The basic element is the seed and the Originator is Allah, the Almighty. It is clear from this simple example that all earnings of both sinner and saint come from Allah. You can trace the same process in all other exchanges and interactions of life. All the metals, gold and silver, from the depths of the earth or the sea are His creation, alone. These are sources of wealth and their Originator is Allah.

The seed is one example of that which Allah has benefited His creation with. The talent with which the carpenter is endowed and with which he fashions doors, windows, tables and beds from wood is the gift of Allah and it is His creation. Mankind's origin is from clay which has become a living human being after Allah breathed into it. It is the will of Allah that it 'Be' and so it 'Is'. All creation is subject to Allah.

One can hardly imagine the wealth which comes from this one object, the seed, Allah's gift. From it has sprung the wealth of nations who specialise in particular commodities or cereals such as wheat, sesame, durra, varieties of fruits and vegetables, cotton and timber, both for local use and export. Both the juice vendor earns as well as the baker.

Let us follow investment and its multiplication a little. From the seed, this primal creation of Allah, emerge trees and thus wood for timber. A carpenter makes, by the will of Allah, chairs, tables, beds, doors, windows and furniture. People buy these necessities. The more they buy, the more his work and business expand. More carpenters will set up in business in order to meet the increased demand, employing more workers. They receive wages with which they buy commodities from the market. The demand for goods increases and so the supply in industries has to increase to meet the demand. More incomes are created. This is the cycle which we can call the multiplier effect in investment.

Be assured that in this cycle usury is not used for the purpose of sustaining the blessing of Allah in the machinery of business. As we noted Allah has prohibited usury in His law in the Glorious Qur'an (2: 275-276, 278-279). The effect of usury is damaging: "Allah deprives usury of all blessing ..." (Qur'an 2: 276), e.g. by the spread of diseases and pests in animals, agriculture and among the populace. So keeping clear of usury will lead to the flourishing of all aspects of business. Increase in industry will lead to an increase in the national income which reflects an increase in the per capita income of the nation or the global community. This all starts from the simple activity of the seed, one of Allah's creations. There are other examples and by considering all of them one can see clearly how all income and all gain stem from natural resources which are from Allah, the Exalted. The increase in gross national income reflects an increase in the per capita income. In the seed, this tiny element of Allah's creation, one sees clearly Allah's power in its true perspective. He is the Giver of Sustenance to all beings.

"Truly Allah is the Ever-Providing, the Steadfast Possessor of Strength."

(Qur'an 51: 58).

We have seen one dimension of economic growth in per capita income and thus national income, all due to this tiny example of Allah's creation, the seed. We have assumed that our hypothetical nation does not indulge in usury. We can take other examples, such as the minerals, iron, nickel, cobalt, copper and lead. If we examine them all carefully, we see clearly that all provision comes from natural resources, which we can all readily understand are from Allah. Allah gives sustenance. All comes from Allah, whether it is the bread, vegetables, fruit, which we eat, sell or trade, whether it is raw, and thus *natural*, or tinned, and thus *processed*, whether it be on an individual, social or national level.

"Say, 'Who provides for you from the heaven and the earth?'"

(Qur'an 10: 31).

"To Him belong the keys of the heavens and the earth. He expands the provision to whomever He wills and He measures out. Truly He is of all things fully knowing."

(Qur'an 42: 12).

"And in the alternation of night and day and in that which Allah sends down from the heaven of sustenance (rain), so that He revives by it the earth after its death, and in the changing of the winds, there are signs for people who use their intelligence."

(Qur'an 45: 5).

"Or who created the heavens and the earth and sent down to you from the sky water, then with it We cause to grow well-planted orchards full of beauty and delight? It is not in your power to cause the growth of their trees. Is there a god with Allah? No, they are people who swerve from justice."

(Qur'an 27: 60).

"And in the heaven is your sustenance and that which you are promised."

(Qur'an 51: 22).

SEED GERMINATION

The seed planted under the ground grows by His will. The conditions for its growth are the water necessary, oxygen, a fertile soil and then the act of germination. Let us look at statements Allah, the Exalted, makes in the Qur'an:

"Have you considered the seed that you sow in the ground? Do you cause it to grow or are We the cause?" (Qur'an 5: 63-64).

"He is the One who produces gardens trellised and untrellised, and date-palms and tilth with produce of all kinds, and olives and pomegranates, similar and different. Eat of their fruit in their season, but render the dues that are proper on the day that the harvest is gathered. And do not waste (by excess). Truly, He does not love those who waste."

(Qur'an 6: 141).

"He is the One who sends down from the sky water for you, from which you drink and from which you have bushes upon which you let your cattle graze and by which He grows for you crops and olives and date-palms and vines and all manner of fruit. Truly in that there are signs for people who reflect."

(Qur'an 16: 10-11).

The seed develops into a plant by the will of Allah. The following is from a work on botany – a brief introduction to plant biology in:

Seed Dormancy and Generation:[5]

"Seeds can remain viable for remarkably long periods. In one study begun in 1788, Dr. W. J. Beal of Michigan State University buried jars containing seeds from several plant species. At 5 and 10 year intervals a jar was opened and the seeds tested for germination. Most species remained viable for at least 10 years, and one species, the Moth Mullein (*Verbascum blattaria*) still germinated after more than 90 years. This however, is no record for seed longevity. Seeds from oriental Lotus (*Nelumbo nucifera*) have been removed, still viable, from archaeological diggings known to be more than 1,000 years old!

"Seeds of a few other species have been recovered from cold anaerobic deposits, dated at over 100 years old, and have also proved viable. <u>It is truly remarkable that seeds can remain living over such long periods</u>."[6]

This ability of the seed to remain viable for long periods has attracted my attention too, and it is quite vividly clear to me that it is not only the creation of the seed in which the will of Allah is the vital determining factor but also in that He wills the seed to germinate.

"Do you cause it to grow, or are We the cause?" (Qur'an 56: 54).

Our author continues, "What induces germination? Many seeds will germinate when provided with moisture, oxygen and a favourable temperature."[19]

But sometimes these elements prove not to be enough. Many seeds will not germinate even when supplied with water, oxygen and a favourable temperature, as the same botany reference implies.

It should be noted that the will of Allah clearly is the determinant factor. This act of will, which permits the seed to grow, to develop and to germinate, is of vital importance. The situation is much the same as the success that the egg has, once successfully fertilised, in developing, implanting itself in the lining of the womb, and becoming an embryo. The elements described as necessary for seed germination require certain balanced conditions. From where can we obtain these conditions, with everything in the proportions required? The seed normally germinates and develops underground, barred from eyesight. Some need light too. There may be millions and billions of seeds in any given landscape. The will of Allah is conspicuous in the whole life-cycle, which starts with birth and ends with death.

Allah states in the Qur'an that He alone permits germination of the seed, and brings forth life from the dead, and the dead from life:

"Truly Allah is the splitter (in germination) of the seed and the date-stone. He brings the living from the dead and He is the bringer of the dead from the living. That is Allah. So how then are you deceived?" (Qur'an 6: 95).

Accumulation of information has to be imbued with faith and nourished with contemplation of the creation of Allah. Then information may result in knowledge, which is an intelligent aim and a lucrative result.

CHAPTER THREE

The Sperm

People, whether laymen, philosophers, scientists, men of talent, kings, emperors, and even prophets, have never been able to create, and never will, one of the key creations, the 'sperm'. It is undoubtedly beyond the power of the human being to create the sperm from which comes human and animal creation.

"And that He created the two of a pair the male and the female from a drop when it is ejaculated."

(Qur'an 53: 45-46).

Thus it is obvious that two of the key origins of life-forms, the seed and the sperm, are inescapably the exclusive creation of Allah. They serve as clear and conspicuous examples, showing that there is a limited jurisdiction for the human being, determined by his Creator.

In the Qur'an, in order to remind us of His creation, Allah refers to the sperm or semen that a man ejaculates into the female to generate the human cycle of life.

"Do you consider that which you ejaculate, do you create it or are We the creators?"

(Qur'an 56: 58-59).

We shall trace this physiological process from one of the reference works on biology to see further the sequence of development. Then we shall contrast those steps of development with what Allah says in the Qur'an. He alone knows what is in the wombs. Scientific knowledge of the process has been permitted to people, later on and after the sending of the prophets. There is a saying of the Prophet, *salla'llahu alaihi wa sallam*, which reflects some knowledge about the foetus. It is a long *hadith* and I have chosen the relevant part.

It is related that Thawban, the freed slave of the Messenger of Allah, *salla'llahu alaihi wa sallam*, said, ...

"He (a Jew) said (to the Prophet), 'I have come to ask you about a thing which no-one amongst the people of the earth knows except a Messenger or one or two besides him.'

"He (the Prophet) said, 'Would it benefit you if I told you that?'

"He (the Jew) said, 'I would bend ears to that,' and he then said, 'I have come to ask you about the child.'

"He (the Prophet) said, 'The reproductive substance of man is white and that of woman[1] yellow, and when they have sexual intercourse and the male's substance[2] prevails upon the female substance[3], it is the male child that is created by the decree of Allah. When the substance of the female prevails upon the substance contributed by the male, then a female child is formed by the decree of Allah.'

"The Jew said, 'What you have said is true. Truly you are a Messenger.' He then turned and went away.'

"The Messenger of Allah, *salla'llahu alaihi wa sallam*, said, 'He asked me about such and such things of which I had no knowledge until Allah gave it to me.' "[4]

The Seed and the Sperm

Besides knowledge about the gender of the child, the Prophet, *salla'llahu alaihi wa sallam*, stated that the offspring is produced by the contributions of both the male and the female, the male reproductive substance (sperm) and the female reproductive substance (ovum).

In another *hadith* the Prophet, *salla'llahu alaihi wa sallam*, said, "The child is not from all of the fluid."[5] It is indeed only one out of the millions of spermatozoa that is the one which actually fertilises the egg.

Let us return to what the Prophet, *salla'llahu alaihi wa sallam*, said, "If the male substance prevails it is a male child that is created, by Allah's decree. When the substance of the female prevails upon the substance contributed by the male then a female child is created, by the decree of Allah."

Examining the physiological picture we find it completely compatible with the *hadith*. Let me clarify that with the following quotation:

"The following is an outline of how the process works. The female possesses a pair of chromosomes that are, arbitrarily, designated as **xx**; the male possesses another pair designated as **xy**. Since the number of chromosomes is reduced (meiosis) during the formation of reproductive cells the spermatozoa are divided into two groups. One group contains **x** and the other **y**. If the **x** ovule is fertilised by a spermatozoon carrying an **x**, a female (**xx**) will be formed. If it fertilised by a **y** spermatozoon the result will be a male (**xy**)."[6]

If the substance of the female **x** prevails upon the substance of the male then a female is formed. "If it is fertilised by a **y** spermatozoon, the result will be a male (**xy**)", i.e. the male's substance prevails upon the female's substance and then it is the male child that is created by the will of Allah.

Proper examination of the data accords with the content of the saying of the Prophet, *salla'llahu alaihi wa sallam*. We shall see also how it coincides with the Qur'an's account of embryonic development. When scientific data does not coincide with the picture painted by the Qur'an, then there is something in the research which needs to be examined more carefully. This is particularly true when the researcher has the vested interest of being a militant atheist trying to extinguish the evidence of the existence of the Creator, glory be to Him high above what they ascribe. Every thing must have an origin, and for all things there is the Originator, the Creator of the heavens and the earth and all that is in between.

He guides and misguides as He wills and according to His perfect indisputable knowledge of His creation. "Doesn't He know whom He has created? And He is the All-Subtle, the All-Aware."

(Qur'an 67: 14).

The misguided ones here refers to those who disbelieve. This, being misguided, can be traced in most theoretical disciplines, e.g.:

1. Economics. The theories of investment and of the rate of interest which are blatantly usurious, and, as we have seen, usury is forbidden by the law of Allah.

2. Literature. It has become full of absolutely bizarre beliefs, distorted values and obscenity.

3. Political theory. It is built on repugnant foundations and a false anti-monotheistic view which affirms a multiplicity of powers in existence, which in short is

polytheism or *shirk* in Arabic. It is based on 'the peo-ple', the sovereignty of the mob, glory be to Allah who is the only All-Powerful One, the True Sovereign. They give sovereignty and they take it through the ballot box. They believe in the constitutions and laws emerg-ing from their public institutions, parliaments, etc., which represent this sovereign. This conception took the stage to a great extent after the upheaval of the French Revolution, 1789, and the Russian Revolution of 1917 against the Tsar. The parliamentary systems, which increased in number hugely over the period be-tween these two events and after the latter, became the forums where laws were debated into legislation while the laws of Allah were shelved.

4. Sociology and Psychology. I have already referred to these in the introduction and, with more elabora-tion, in my book on Western literature in the light of Islamic ethics.[7]

The believers know that all power is from Allah and all sovereignty belongs to Him, to the extent that even their going astray is from His decree, for He guides whom He wills and misguides whom He wills. Allah alone is the Ultimate Sovereign. He gives sovereignty and takes it as He wills. The believers know that the law is truly Allah's alone, from His revealed books, the only valid and up-to-date one of which is the Qur'an. The only ones who may produce a law are the prophets, who bring it by revelation from the Divine. They are the ones whose own personal conduct and their own sayings outside of the revealed speech of Allah, do not conflict with that revelation, rather they embody it most perfectly. The whole is a complete package of revelation for human beings to live by, to worship and to pave the way to the Garden, rather than the constitutions and laws of this age. Those who do not comply with, and rule by, this revealed law are "those who disbelieve," "the unjust", "the corrupt".

"And whoever does not judge (rule) by that which Allah has revealed, then those, they are the unbelievers." "And whoever does not judge (rule) by that which Allah has revealed, then those, they are the unjust." "And whoever does not judge (rule) by that which Allah has revealed, then those, they are the corrupt." (Qur'an 5: 44-45, 47).

Any laws contrary to the law of Allah are invalid, and the people who abide by them are merely following their own caprices. They are astray and on a path which leads to the Fire.

The examples we are treating, i.e. the seed and the sperm and the whole subject matter of this book, are being dealt with in order that the reader might go from belief to certainty. Then, perhaps, by the will of Allah, a colossal change might occur, which is turning to Allah and moving towards uprightness.

In the fields of science, deviation is not quite as blatant nor as obvious as it is in other theoretical subjects such as philosophy, except with those militant atheists who do not confine themselves to observation and collection of data, but force a philosophical interpretation on data, and who do not believe in the Creator but believe only in the spontaneous and causeless growth of things. Or they believe that, due to favourable physical circumstances, compounds were spontaneously able to combine together in an organised fashion, and, by uniting, were able to produce the wonderful complexity of the creation that is the cell and from there even more complex living organisms. They believe everything can be explained by postulating the all-pervading power of natural selection.

If we examine the world we live in, and our own lives, very carefully, we find that everything is organised and planned to the finest detail and that all component parts of creation are inter-related. How is it possible then to imagine that the whole of creation came into existence by a tremendous accident, and that it continues to develop by spontaneous reactions without an overall design and designer? The sun, the moon, the stars, the heavens, the earth we live on, the rivers and mountains, all sprang spontaneously into being?!

The sun rises in the east and sets in the west and the moon begins its cycles as the crescent of the new moon, waxes to become the full moon and then wanes until it is the thin crescent moon again. How can this cosmos which evinces design down to the tiniest most insignificant detail not arouse the conviction in us of the eternal presence of the Creator? For by Him are the regular and enduring, well-calculated solar orbit and rotation of the earth which cause the alternation of night and day and the seasons.

If nothing else the sheer beauty of it all should so flood our hearts as to arouse awareness of the Divine presence. How wonderful it is to see darkness fading away at moon-rise to be followed by the bright moon-lit night radiant with beaming light. For all things upon earth have an originator and the Originator of the originators is One.

If one considers one's own creation, from conception in the womb, through the development of the embryo, birth and the later development of the child until it reaches adulthood, one finds that it all takes place in perfectly organised stages. This is true of all life-forms, animals, birds, fish and plants. This sequence of events from the fertilisation of the egg through its subsequent development is clear proof, for whoever has eyes to see, of the One Designer and Creator of all things. We say that none are so blind as those who refuse to see, none so deaf as those who refuse to hear. A guilty conscience needs no accuser. Indeed Allah has created some hearts dumb, and we don't blame eyes that do not see. The All-Knowing says, "The eyes are not blind, but rather it is the hearts in the breasts which are blind." (Qur'an 22: 46).

We will quote some examples from the Qur'an, the true words of Allah, and compare them with observational data of the matter of reproduction, in order to make clear the presence of the Originator, the Creator, the Organiser, the All-Powerful who is able to do all things. Perhaps, some people, by reading that which they did not know before may surrender to Allah in Islam. One is never too old to learn, for the Prophet, *salla'llahu alaihi wa sallam*, ordered us to "Seek knowledge from the cradle to the grave." So repair yourself, put it right without despair.

It is important to note that the major steps of development coincide in both observational data and in the Qur'an. Observation goes into minute detail on some matters. Comparing the two, the alert and wise person will only find it obvious that knowledge is from

The Seed and the Sperm

Allah. "And you have not been given of knowledge but a little." (Qur'an 17: 85).

Qur'an is the base of all our knowledge and it is the only absolute reference. If one does not find complete coherence or coincidence between observation, experiment and the Qur'an, there must be an error in the observation or experiment.

First, let us dwell on the process of development of the human being. After ejaculation the semen normally finds its way to the womb. One sperm out of millions fuses with the ovum (egg). This is the first phase of fertilisation.

In the second step this fusion of sperm and egg produces a zygote, the first cell, which then clings to the wall of the uterus. This implantation is a very vital and crucial step for the success of the development. This is pregnancy. If the zygote does not cling, the result is failure, or miscarriage. It becomes the implanted **blood-clot** clinging to the wall of the uterus, and the phase of embryonic development begins, until it becomes a **foetus**. It completes the normal period of nine months and is pushed out into the world as a healthy baby. This is the simple description of the process of the steps of development.

Now let me quote from a reference by a biologist to show the development. It is worth noting that the specialist doesn't know the Qur'anic *ayats*. I mention this to underscore the parity between the Qur'an and observational and experimental data, the origin being one – all knowledge is from Allah, the All-Knowing, and is only allowed by Him to whom He chooses and, rightly seen, leads to Him.

THE PROCESS OF DEVELOPMENT

Reproduction[8]

"During copulation (often called sexual intercourse in humans), the male introduces **sperm** in the body of the female; this permits fertilisation to occur inside the female's body rather than in an external, and possibly unfavourable, environment. Depending on the species, the resulting embryo may develop internally, or the female may lay a fertilised egg.

Pregnancy

"Sperm released in the vagina during ejaculation swim through the cervix and uterus into the fallopian tubes, [I prefer 'uterine tubes' since it is arrogant to name Allah's creation after human beings e.g. Fallopian tubes, Langhan cells, hurricane Angela, etc.] where fertilisation usually occurs.

(This description of pregnancy applies primarily to humans, but the situation is similar in other mammals.)

"The fertilised egg, already undergoing development, moves slowly down into the uterus. About a week after fertilisation, it starts to **cling to** the endometrium of the uterus. The most important organ of pregnancy then begins to form. This is the placenta produced partly by the uterine wall and partly by the embryo.

Fertilisation

"Fertilisation is the reaction between the haploid sperm and a haploid egg that produces a diploid zygote.

"Fusion of the gametes at fertilisation: an egg (the

83

female gamete contains food for the embryo and molecules that control early development. As a result of all this luggage, an egg is too large to be mobile and must sit around waiting to be found. A mobile sperm is the necessary complement to the non-mobile egg, and the two have evolved together) produces a single-cell zygote that is not equipped to live as its multicellular parents live until it has undergone a period of embryonic development. At first, it must divide and form many cells. Secondly, cells must **differentiate** from one another, taking on different shapes and chemical characteristics that specialise them for their later roles in different parts of the body. Thirdly, the embryonic cells must move around, spread out, or clump together, creating the many different assemblages of cells that give each organ, and the body as a whole, its characteristic form. While all this is going on, the embryo is supplied with food either from the egg yolk, or by exchange of food between, the maternal and foetal bloodstreams (as in most mammals), or by a combination of the two.

"Fertilisation is a complicated case of two cells recognising one another, whether fertilisation is internal, within the female's body, or external, in water surrounding fluid. When a sperm touches the jelly around the egg, it sticks there. Apparently a certain amount of this substance must be neutralised by single sperms before any sperm can penetrate the jelly to reach the egg. A single sperm can probably never fertilise an egg by itself; thousands of sperms usually stick to the jelly coat before fertilisation can occur. When enough sperm are stuck to the egg, the sperms' active role ends and the egg takes over. The egg membrane engulfs the head of a sperm and pulls the sperm nucleus into the egg, leaving the rest of the sperm outside. As soon as this happens, some sort of electrical and chemical reaction runs throughout the egg cell membrane and makes it impermeable to further sperm.

Embryonic Development

"Embryonic development is a complex process involving cell division, cell differentiation and cell movement as the genetic information in the zygote expresses itself and forms the mature animal. In order to understand just how complex this process is, let us consider three major aspects of development.

"The first of these is differentiation into cell types.

"From one fertilised zygote, which is one type of cell, cells as different as liver, muscle, nerve and skin cells are produced. These cells, differ from one another in that they have synthesised different enzymes and structural proteins.

"This must be due to the fact that different genes have become active in different cells during development.

"The second aspect of embryonic development is growth.

"How and why do cells divide and grow? At various stages in development, depending on the animal, food from outside reaches the embryo and enables it to increase its overall size. The mammalian embryo is nourished by the placenta, a tadpole hatches into a frog which eats for itself. Before this point, no overall growth occurs, however, the number of cells in the embryo has increased enormously by cell division.

The Seed and the Sperm

Formation of Shapes

"This consists, on a molecular level, of the rearrangement of proteins and other molecules to form larger structures within cells and, on a larger scale, of the movement and building of cells into specific patterns to form organs.

"By the end of the third week the embryo has entered the stage of organogenesis. In this stage the major organ systems begin to form the nervous system, gut and blood vessels. The heart shaped like a lumpy tube, starts to pulsate.

"During the third month, the **foetus** begins to move, and the mother may feel its movements. From this point onwards the most obvious progress is growth in size."[9]

Birth

"In humans, the date of birth averages 270 days after conception, but there is much variation in the time a baby takes to develop."[10]

We can see several major aspects of the above quotations: **the semen or spermatozoa, the zygote, the clinging of the blood clot, differentiation of the single cell into cells, the embryo and the foetus, leading to birth at a later point**.

The following *ayah* from the Qur'an shows the major steps of the process of human development.

"O mankind, if you are in doubt as to the resurrection, then truly We created you of dust, then of a **drop**[11], then of a **blood-clot**[12], then of **a lump of flesh**, formed and unformed[13], that We may make clear to you. And

86

We establish in the wombs what We will, till a **stated term**[14], then We deliver you as **infants**[15], then that you may come of age, and some of you die, and some of you are kept back unto the most decrepit state of life (old age and senility), that after knowing somewhat, they may know nothing. And you behold the earth blackened, then, when We send down water upon it, **it quivers and swells and puts forth herbage of every joyous kind."**

(Qur'an 22: 5).

The literal translation of the stage after the drop (the sperm) is **the clinging blood-clot** as I clarified in the footnotes to show the exact literal translation of the Arabic word (*ʿalaqah*); which is very important indeed in the comparison between observational evidence and the Qur'an.

The human process of development is beautifully compared with the arid dead earth receiving water which then shakes, becomes lively and brings out new life. The comparison shows that the Creator is One, and the idea or process the same. The womb and the earth are likened; semen is emitted into the womb, and the water falls from the sky, sent down by Allah to the earth. The bringing forth of life in the womb through the fertilisation of the egg by sperm, and the generation cycle which then takes place until an offspring is delivered, is like the water coming to an arid, lifeless land which then quivers into life again bringing forth beautiful species and crops of plants, flowers and fruits. The comparison is really marvellous. The resemblance between the two processes, so widely differing in their outward natures, indicates the Oneness of the

The Seed and the Sperm

Originator of both. In another extraordinary *ayah* Allah extends the same analogy: "Your women are a tilth to you, so approach your tilth however you will."
(Qur'an 2: 223).

We can see clearly the comparison between the Qur'anic *ayah* and the observational evidence. The steps are the same. The Qur'anic steps are very exact; their order is very precise. It is clear that the Qur'an is the speech of Allah because the facts are so well organised.

The steps are very exact and the *ayats* contain concise information. In the disciplines based upon observation and experiment, the description must rigorously follow the steps so that one step doesn't precede another in the wrong order. Sometimes in the Qur'an, the Creator suffices by giving the general picture of something, at other times, treating of the same topic He may give a more or less detailed picture. Yet one can never find the chronological sequence changing, e.g. the clinging of the *alaqah* (the blood-clot) never comes at a later stage than the embryo or before the 'drop' (the sperm). But sometimes the step of the 'drop' (the sperm) is missed out and the major process of the blood-clot, the clinging blood-clot is alone referred to as an inevitable process of creation. Because if it didn't cling there would be abortion and miscarriage. The mention of *alaqah* (the blood-clot) alone signifies how vital it is in the process of the life of the human being.

The interesting question, for those who insist on viewing the Qur'an as the work of the Prophet Muhammad, *salla'llahu alaihi wa sallam*, is, how could he know these steps, at a time when, particularly among the desert Arabs, dissection of the body, the study of anatomy, physiology, and surgery and all its techniques and technology were not as they are today?

CHAPTER FOUR

Reproduction, Fate and Destiny
IN SOME OF THE SAYINGS
OF THE PROPHET

The Messenger of Allah, *salla'llahu alaihi wa sallam*, knew, by Allah's guidance much, in addition to what was revealed to him through the Qur'an, as we saw in the report of the encounter with the Jew. There are other sayings of the Prophet, *salla'llahu alaihi wa sallam*, in which Allah has guided him to the truth of a situation, for example, those sayings in which he spoke further on the development of the child and his destiny. Of that there is the remarkable fact that our destinies have been written since our earliest moments and known to Allah alone in their most minute details, whether we were to be happy or miserable, saints or criminals and rich or poor.

Allah, the Exalted, says, "Every human being, We have fastened his fate on his neck and We will bring out for him on the Day of Resurrection a book which he will see spread open, 'Read your book. Sufficient is your own self on this day as a reckoner against you.'"

(Qur'an, Al-Isra: 13-14).

Yet this knowledge of fate or destiny no mortal being can know it whatever other knowledge he has been given, because Allah alone knows what He decrees when the foetus is in the womb. That secret knowledge of Allah is not only the rather trivial matter of whether the infant is male or female, a simple thing which can be determined mechanically rather simply through ultra-sound scanning. Some rather simple-minded people imagine that this technology contradicts the words of Allah, when He says, "Truly Allah, with Him is the knowledge of the Hour (of the Last Day). He sends down the rain, and He knows what is in the wombs. Nor does anyone know that which they will earn on the morrow. Nor does anyone know in which land he will die. Truly Allah is all-knowing, fully aware."

(Qur'an 31: 34).

The Prophet Muhammad, *salla'llahu alaihi wa sallam*, also said, "No-one knows that which the wombs will be pregnant with except Allah."[1]

Imagine that parents could know, when their children were born, what would be the destinies and the futures of these children, e.g. they knew that when the newly born child grows up he will be a major criminal. They would quite possibly get rid of him at birth. Suppose, on the other hand, they found out that their baby would be one day a prince or a king or a wealthy man or an extremely poor man: one could imagine the different types of reaction they would have. Then think of the son of the Prophet Nuh, *alaihi's-salaam*, who was drowned at the time of the great flood, while Nuh was pleading with Allah to save his son from drowning with the other infidels: "So the ship (the Ark) floated with them on the waves which were like mountains, and Nuh called out to his son, who had separated himself, 'O my son! Embark with us and don't be with the ones who disbelieve.'

91

The Seed and the Sperm

"He (his son) said, 'I will take myself to some mountain which will save me from the water.'

"Nuh said, 'This day nothing can save from the command of Allah except for whomever He showed mercy.' And the waves came between them and the son was among those who were drowned."

(Qur'an, Surah Hud: 42-43).

"And Nuh called upon his Lord and said, 'O my Lord, surely my son is of my family. And Your promise is true and You are the most just of judges.'

"He (Allah) said, 'O Nuh, he was not of your family. He is an incorrect action, so do not ask Me about that of which you have no knowledge. I warn you lest you act like one of the ignorant.'

"He said, 'O my Lord, I seek refuge with You lest I should ask You something about which I have no knowledge. And if You don't forgive me and show mercy to me I shall be one of the losers.'"

(Qur'an, Surah Hud: 45-46).

So one can imagine that if such secrets, of the destinies of one's children, were known in advance, how much life would be in constant turmoil. Allah alone knows what is in the wombs in that sense, rather than in the mere sense of the gender of the foetus. This knowledge of destiny has been screened completely from all beings, except for the Creator, who, of course, knows about what He has created, their fates, their life-spans, their provisions and whether they will be ultimately happy or miserable, i.e. in the Garden or in the Fire. "Doesn't He who created know? And He is the Subtle, the All-Aware."

(Qur'an 67: 14).

"Say, 'Praise belongs to Allah the One who has not taken a son, nor is there a partner to Him in the kingdom, nor is there a protecting friend for Him from humiliation,' and magnify Him greatly."
(Qur'an 17: 111).

Allah is All-Powerful over everything. His command, when He wills something to be, only is that He says to it 'Be' and it 'Is'. There is none who shares with Him in His sovereignty and rule. To Him is all the praise.

Some sayings of the Prophet, *salla'llahu alaihi wa sallam*, give an account of the process of development and of Allah's knowledge of that which is in the wombs, whether it be for good or evil.[2]

The narrator of the following *hadith* heard Abdullah Ibn Masoud, *radiya'llahu anhu*, saying, "The miserable one one is he who is miserable in the womb of his mother, and the happy one is he who draws lessons from the fate of others."

The narrator (of the *hadith*) came to a person from amongst the companions of the Messenger of Allah, *salla'llahu alaihi wa sallam*, who was called Hudhayfa ibn Usaid al-Ghifari and narrated to him what he had heard Ibn Masoud say, then he said, "How can a person be miserable without committing a deed?"

Thereupon the companion said to him, "You are surprised at this, whereas I have heard the Messenger of Allah, *salla'llahu alaihi wa sallam*, saying, 'When forty-two nights pass after the drop (of semen) enters the womb, Allah sends the angel to it and he gives the child its shape, then he creates his sense of hearing, sense of sight, his skin, his flesh, his bones and then says, "My Lord, should he be male or female?" And your Lord

93

decides as He desires. And the angel records that also, and then says, "My Lord, what about his life-span?" And your Lord decides as He desires. And the angel records that. Then he says, "My Lord, what about his provision?" And the Lord decides as He desires. And the angel records it. The angel comes out with the child's scroll of destiny in his hand and nothing is added to it, and nothing is subtracted from it.'"

Anas ibn Malik, *radiya'llahu anhu*, reported directly from the Messenger of Allah, *salla'llahu alaihi wa sallam*, that he said, "Allah, the Exalted and Glorious, has appointed an angel as the guardian of the womb, and he says, 'My Lord it is now a drop (of semen). My Lord it is now a blood-clot. My Lord it has now become a lump of flesh.' When Allah has decided to give it its final shape, the angel asks, 'My Lord will it be a male or a female? Will it be an evil or a good person? What about its livelihood and its life-span?' It is all written down as the baby is in the womb of its mother."

Notice that the progress of the development in the *hadith* is the same as in the Qur'an and as noted in observation.

Ali, *radiya'llahu anhu*, reported that, "One day we were sitting with the Messenger of Allah, *salla'llahu alaihi wa sallam*, and he had a piece of wood in his hand and he was scratching the ground. He raised his head and said, 'There is no-one among you who has not been allotted his seat in the Garden or the Fire.'

"They said, 'Messenger of Allah, then why should we do good deeds? Why not depend upon our destinies?'

"Thereupon he said, 'No, perform good actions, for everyone is eased to that for which he has been created.' Then he recited this *ayah* of Qur'an, 'Then as for he who gives and guards against evil and affirms the best [Islam – author's note], so We will ease him to the greatest ease. And as for he who is mean and thinks himself independent [turns away from the perfect religion – author's note] and denies the very best, so We will ease him to the most difficult.'

(Qur'an, Surat al-Layl: 5-10)"[3]

All of the aforementioned explanation about destiny, as related in the *hadith* of the Messenger of Allah, *salla'llahu alaihi wa sallam*, is said in very precise and exact words by Allah, the Exalted, "We decide in the wombs whatever We will."

(Qur'an, Surat al-Hajj: 5)

There is another explanation for the exclusive knowledge that Allah has of that which is in the wombs. As we have seen the sperm fertilises the ovum which becomes then a zygote. Then in the form of the blood-clot (*ᶜalaqah*) it clings to the wall of the uterus in this first stage of embryonic development. Then it grows into the foetus. There is of course an increase in the womb through this first growth. If the blood-clot fails to cling, then there is a miscarriage and henceforth a decrease in the womb. The decision as to whether the mother will have a baby or not rests entirely with Allah alone. Whether there will be an increase or a decrease in the womb only Allah knows. It is at precisely this precarious moment of development that the way is open to the embryo to develop into a child or not, but that has been known to Allah alone, from all eternity, from when we were only minute particles in the loins of our ancestors.

The Seed and the Sperm

"And when your Lord took from the children of Adam, from their backs, their descendants and made them witness against themselves, 'Am I not your Lord?'

"They said, 'Certainly, we witness', lest you say on the Day of Resurrection, 'It was only that our ancestors associated partners (with Allah) beforehand [e.g. by saying Jesus is a god or a son of God or a member of the Trinity, or taking idols as gods, or worshipping spirits, or incarnation in any sense or form – author's note] and we were their descendants after them, so would you destroy us for that which men of no faith did?'

"And in that way do we detail the *ayats* in order that they might return."

(Qur'an 7: 172-174).

There is no excuse for those who disbelieve on the Last Day. Allah knows well His creation, both in the ancient times and in the later times.

"Allah knows what every female bears (in pregnancy) and what the wombs decrease (in miscarriage) and what they increase."

(Qur'an 13: 8).

Allah alone knows what the female bears in the womb, a believer or a criminal, a happy one or a miserable one. Sometimes, a miscarriage may have been a great mercy from Allah for the parents, to prevent the birth of a child who might have been a catastrophe for them. We cannot take this to include the use of abortion to escape unwanted and perhaps even illegitimate pregnancy. We refer to miscarriage which is the natural abortion, which may be of benefit to parents, or on the other hand a test of their patience and endurance.

Allah knows well why He gives and withholds; all is His undeniable sovereign power.

There is the famous and very challenging story of a slave of God who killed a child, to the great distress and confusion of Musa, *alaihi's-salaam*, because the child would have grown up to be a misery and affliction for his parents. This is the analogy of the spontaneous natural abortion called miscarriage, which it is conceivable that Allah may cause as a mercy to the parents, and Allah knows best.

"Then they (Musa and the slave of God) proceeded until, when they met a young boy, he (The slave of God) killed the boy. Musa said, 'Have you killed an innocent person who had not killed anyone? Truly you have done a terrible thing.'"

(Qur'an 18: 74).

The slave of God's answer was, "As for the boy, his parents were people of faith, and we feared that he would grieve them by obstinate rebellion and ingratitude (*kufr*). So we desired that their Lord would give them in exchange one better than him in purity of conduct and closer in affection."

(Qur'an 18: 80-81).

We must emphasise that this deed was done by one who was instructing a prophet, one who received his knowledge from Allah. No person could be allowed to take upon himself the responsibility for such an act, out of surmise or imagination. Even a prophet will not kill a person except for a clear criminal offence and according to the law of Allah and the evidence of clear witnesses. What happened here was an extremely unusual case, special to those persons in that time, and could not be permitted again. I have only quoted this famous story to show that Allah may prevent the birth of a child, through the much more ordinary and everyday event of miscarriage, natural abortion, for reasons which are beyond our comprehension.

We have seen that wombs increase after the success of fertilisation, and the clinging of the blood-clot. This is a determining and crucial factor in the early development, to the extent that Allah, the Exalted, will often skip mention of the preceding stages and refers only to the *ᶜalaqah*, which we have called 'the clinging blood-clot'. He, the Exalted, even named an entire *surah*, the one which contains the very first verses revealed, *Al-ᶜAlaq*, It begins, "Read in the name of your Lord who created, created man from an *ᶜalaq*." (Qur'an 96: 1-2).

THE INFORMANT IS ONE, THE ONE GOD

As we have seen before, the *ayats* of the Qur'an, which are Allah's revelations, and the *hadith* of the Prophet, *salla'llahu alaihi wa sallam*, which are his recorded sayings, go step-by-step in agreement with the processes of reproduction described and recorded by biologists, physiologists, obstetricians and gynaecologists. Whether the author is a *believer* or an *un-believer*, whether he is aware of what Allah has revealed in the Qur'an or not, one can still trace the same steps of reproduction, because the reality is One, and the description of it is One, whether it is by revelation or observation. Ultimately Allah is the only Informant, He alone, the All-Knowing. He has permitted some to know the details of certain principles of knowledge already mentioned in the Qur'an, such as the details of the *salah* (prayer), the fast, the *zakah* tax on wealth for the poor and needy, and the *hajj* pilgrimage to Makkah, and even mathematics, and astronomy.

The details of the acts of worship and the laws of the *shariah* are given to chosen people, called prophets, through revelation. Ordinary human beings are permitted details of knowledge through means of observation, experimentation, reflection and thought. Among such people there are scientists who have specialised in mathematics, physics, chemistry, botany, biology, etc., of the practical sciences. Read the statement of Allah in the Qur'an to clarify this, and to clarify the overwhelming power that He has over everything:

"He is the one who made the sun a radiance and the moon a light and measured it (the moon) in phases in order that you might know the number of the years and the reckoning. Allah did not create that except with truth. We detail the *ayats* for a people who have knowledge."

(Qur'an 10: 5).

The heart, the brain and the senses are marvellous creations of Allah, and they are our instruments of perception and cognition. No-one can claim credit for, or ownership of, their own knowledge. Let us refer to the case of Qaroun (Korah in the Bible) who was devastated by Allah for his arrogance and ingratitude.

"Truly Qaroun was of the people of Musa but he acted insolently against them. And We bestowed upon him such treasures that their keys would have been a burden to a body of strong men.

The Seed and the Sperm

"When his people said to him, 'Do not exult, for Allah does not love those who exult. And seek in that which Allah has given you the abode of the next life. And do not forget your portion of this life. And act excellently well as Allah has acted excellently well to you. And do not seek and desire corruption in the land. Truly Allah does not love those who corrupt.'

"He said, 'I have only been given it because of a knowledge which I have.'

"Did he not know that Allah had destroyed before him generations who were superior to him in strength and greater than him in collecting (wealth). Criminals will not be asked about their wrong actions."

(Qur'an 28: 76-78).

"Then We caused the earth to swallow him and his house, and there was not any party who would help him apart from Allah, and he was not one of those helped to victory."

(Qur'an 28: 81).

Allah gives knowledge to whom He chooses, even His enemies who are destroyed by attributing it to themselves and not seeing it as the gift of Allah, the All-Knowing, to them. The One who gives knowledge, or even information, the Informant is Allah alone, the Knower of every thing, the Creator, the Sovereign and the Lord of all beings.

"And He taught Adam the names, all of them, and then He showed them to the angels and said, 'Inform me of the names of these if you are truthful.'

"They said, 'Glory be to You. We have no knowledge except that which You have taught us. Truly You are the All-Knowing, the Completely-Wise.'

"He said, 'O Adam, tell them their names.'

"So that when he had informed them of their names, He said, 'Did I not say to you that I know the unseen of the heavens and the earth, and I know what you make manifest and what you used to conceal?'"

(Qur'an 2: 31-33).

Allah revealed in the Qur'an the story of the two brothers who both offered sacrifices to Allah. Allah accepted the sacrifice of one of them and not that of the other. The second brother become jealous of the first, the righteous brother and killed him. He did not know what to do with the corpse. Allah sent a crow, which by its nature digs the ground and buries things, and it showed him what to do with the body of his brother. He imitated the crow and dug a section of earth in which he placed the body of his brother and then covered it over with soil.

Allah, the Exalted, says, "So Allah sent a crow, which scratched at the earth (hiding remains it carried in its beak in the ground) to show him how to hide the naked body of his brother. He said, 'Woe is me! Was I not even able to be as this crow and to conceal the corpse of my brother?' and then he became one of the regretful."

(Qur'an 5: 31).

This was one means by which Allah conveyed knowledge. It was teaching the man through his observation. All means of research, teaching, observation and experimentation are ways to seek inspiration from Allah as to the truth of things, if they are carried out in the right spirit and in accord with the Qur'an and the Sunnah. But one must remember that Allah guides and misleads according to His knowledge of His creatures:

"Does He who created not know? And He is the All-Subtle, the All-Aware."

(Qur'an 67: 14).

"Say, 'Truly Allah misleads whomever He wills and He guides to Himself whoever turns in penitence.'"

(Qur'an 13: 27).

"For truly Allah misleads whomever He wills and He guides whomever He wills."

(Qur'an 35: 8).

Where knowledge is not in conformity with Allah's revealed way, the Qur'an and the Sunnah, then it is misguidance. Allah knows well His creatures. Most of the theoretical bases in different fields such as economics, sociology and psychology, for example, need to be subjected to the most careful scrutiny. There are already strong roots for these disciplines in the Qur'an and the Sunnah, and there were in the previous revelations, the Torah and the Gospels, before they were altered. One is undoubtedly astray if one abandons, as one's bases, an already sure revealed knowledge for painstaking trial and error, groping in the dark and speculation. A strong trust and belief in Allah and a good knowledge of the Qur'an and the Sunnah enable one to pass through life and its many trials safely without the extra difficulty of stumbling in thought and wandering far on divergent paths.

Abdullah Ibn Masoud, *radiya'llahu anhu*, narrated that the Prophet, *salla'llahu alaihi wa sallam*, once made a line on the ground with his hand and said, "This is the straight path of Allah." Then he made other lines to the right and to the left of the main path and said, "On each of these paths there is a *Shaytan* (Satan) calling to it." Then he read out Allah's statement in the Qur'an, "And this is My path, straight, so follow it and do not follow divergent paths lest they should scatter you from His path. That is what He counsels you in order that you might guard yourselves from harm."

(Qur'an 6: 153).[4]

These divergent paths are often found to have Shaytans in human form calling to them, those who do not take guidance from the revelation and thus mislead others. There are so many historical examples of leaders and thinkers who have lead millions astray, e.g. Marx, Engels, Lenin, Rousseau, Spinoza, Keynes (a propagator, from among a long line of philosophers of economics, of a theory of investment and of the rate of interest which is mega-usurious), Darwin, Freud, Kant, Sartre, Bacon, and Paul of Tarsus who deviated most disastrously the Christian teaching.

This age is characterised by usury above all other evils. Even at the time of Shakespeare it was considered a monstrous deed to give or take interest. For that see *The Merchant of Venice*.[5] In this age the majority of people seek wealth and money with no regard to moral, ethical or religious values. Colossal pyramids of usury-banking have spread all over the world having no regard for revelation or the law of Allah.

Our age has seen an enormous upheaval in ethics, and a complete loss of values in sexual relations, within or without marriage. The author of one of the most recent offerings in this domain, a book called *Ethics!*, admitted that he didn't believe in the existence of God (glory be to Allah who does not need anyone to believe in Him). Yet, even after propagating such stuff, if the person turns from his wrong to Allah, the Real, the Truth, he will find Allah All-Forgiving.

(See Qur'an 5: 74).

The path of those unbelievers, and the path of those who are unjust, is one and the same path, and it leads straight to the Fire. Their philosophies and theories are all designed to lead to such an end. Qur'an contains the most exact science without any equivalent to it anywhere else at all. It is law AND wisdom from the All-Wise, the All-Knowing, Allah the Almighty.

"Truly, the ones who disbelieve and who act unjustly, Allah would not forgive them, nor would He guide them on a path except the path to Jahannam (Hell), therein abiding for ever. That is easy for Allah."

(Qur'an 4: 168-169).

One must not have a shallow picture of good and evil. Shaytan has promised Allah to lead most people astray and he was given sanction to do so and the reward will be the Fire. But Allah is most forgiving for those who do wrong in ignorance and repent before the time of death.

"Turning to Allah in repentance is only for those who do wrong in ignorance then repent soon afterwards. So, those Allah turns to them. And Allah is all-knowing, all-wise."

(Qur'an 4: 17).

The human must always be aware of the fact that his arch-enemy is Shaytan who has promised to Allah, "I will take of Your slaves a portion marked off. I will mislead them and I will create in them false desires."

(Qur'an 4: 118-119).

Allah does not compell people to believe in Him, but He is merciful and compassionate, and He sees the fate that people propel themselves towards. That is the truth, the clear reality. We appeal to Allah, the Almighty, to help us and all people to believe and trust sincerely in Him, and to guide us all on the true and real way which He has blessed. Allah has sent prophets to people and to the Jinn, so that they may be aware of Him, conscious of His presence, and to show them the way to paradise. Allah has created the Jinn and all people only for them to worship Him and be in full submission to Him. Trust in Allah as the Creator is the vital issue, and then servitude to Him alone automatically follows. He repeatedly counsels reflection in order for us to understand how we are created, which will thereby strengthen trust in our hearts.

"Do they not consider the camels and how they were created, the heaven and how it was raised up, the mountains and how they were erected, and the earth and how it was stretched out?"

(Qur'an 88: 17-20).

In the Qur'an, Allah poses a rhetorical question about the sperm which, with desire, is ejaculated into the womb, "Do you create it or are We the creators?"

(Qur'an 56: 59).

Allah is its creator. The real unalterable relation between mankind and Him is that of the slave to the Lord. Allah created the ovum and the sperm. He permitted legitimate marriage between men and women. The creation must not be misused and abused.

"Does man reckon that he will be left purposeless? Was he not a drop of sperm ejaculated, then he was a blood-clot, then He formed and perfected and made of him two of a pair, the male and the female. Is That One not able to make the dead live?"

(Qur'an 75: 36-40).

TO BE OR NOT TO BE

Allah, the Exalted, ordered the Prophet Muhammad, *salla'llahu alaihi wa sallam*, to read the Qur'an. It is the basis for education for generation after generation until the end of time. One reads in order to understand Allah's power and splendour manifest in creation, and to recognise His Oneness and All-Pervading Presence. Allah is the Refuge, the Lord and Supreme King, and the Owner, of everything. He is the Creator.

"In the name of Allah, the Merciful, the Compassionate. Recite! In the name of your Lord who created. He created man from a blood-clot. Recite! And your Lord is the Most Generous who taught by the pen, taught man that which he did not know. No indeed, truly man is insolent that he sees himself independent. Truly, to your Lord is the ultimate return."

(Qur'an 96: 1-8).

With these words "Recite! (or Read!) In the name of your Lord who created. He created man from a blood-clot," began the first revelation to the Prophet Muhammad, *salla'llahu alaihi wa sallam.*

You notice that the reference here is to the clinging blood-clot. The exact Arabic word is ꜥ*alaq.* If one throws a minute blood-clot upon a cloth or a garment, it sticks or clings itself. In reproduction it thus sticks to, and clings to, the wall of the uterus where it then grows and develops.

The placenta also forges a relation between the inner embryo and the outer mother. The embryo receives nourishment through this extraordinary creation. The implanting of the blood-clot is a crucial step in reproduction as we have noted. Without it there would be a miscarriage.

"Recite in the name of your Lord who created. He created man from a blood-clot." The selection of the ʿalaq as a step of development is crucial because Allah has highlighted this in particular through choosing the name of this surah, the ʿalaq .

We can see the importance of this particularly in the light of the following.

TEST-TUBE BABIES

In the ensuing we will assume that the transference of the sperm and the ovum takes place between a legitimate couple of husband and wife. We are here concerned with fact only and to prove that no new creation takes place, because the two elements of life, the sperm and the ovum are clearly the creation of Allah.

"We created you. So what if you do not affirm? Have you considered that which you ejaculate, is it you who create it or are We the creators? We have decreed among you death and We shall not be outstripped from exchanging the likes of you and creating you anew in that which you do not know."

(Qur'an 56: 57-61).

We are also concerned with the sequence in the reproduction process which has been stated by Allah in Surat al-Hajj, ayah 5. This sequence, as we have shown, when compared to observational data, is identical.

The Seed and the Sperm

Sometimes, as we have seen, Allah, the Exalted, refers to the most crucial step in reproduction as the vital step in the process of development, the step of the implanting of the blood-clot within the wall of the uterus.

News of test-tube babies has had an astounding effect on the majority of people who are quite unaware that it is in no way a new creation. It is simply a piece of dexterity by surgeons and other specialists, who do what they do by the will of Allah.

In some cases, the first cycle of reproduction, which takes place in the uterine tube, goes wrong for a variety of reasons. This is one cause of infertility. So physicians in England facilitated the fusion of the sperm and the ovum externally. A sperm, from the semen of the husband, and an ovum, from his wife, united in an external environment at the same ambient temperature as the womb. The fusion of the two gametes took place within laboratory equipment, rather than within the uterine tubes, thus the nickname, 'test-tube babies'. The important point is that this fusion usually happens quite naturally within the uterine tube and results in a zygote. For one reason or another, with some couples the process goes wrong. By their God-given, manual dexterity and by reproducing as far as possible the scientifically observed conditions which naturally occur in the womb, physicians were able to allow this miraculous fusion of sperm and ovum to take place outside of the womb.

But, although fusion occurred outside of the womb, they had to **replace the zygote back into the womb to allow it to implant into the uterine wall. If it had not implanted, it would have spontaneously aborted or**

miscarried. All that matters is the decree of Allah, **to be or not to be**. The implantation within the wall of the uterus is absolutely crucial for this blastocyst for its embryonic development to take place. The words of Allah and the steps outlined in the Qur'an have to be fulfilled. The *ᶜalaq* has to implant in the uterine wall whether the fusion of sperm and ovum takes place within the womb or elsewhere.

The original elements, the sperm and the ovum, are the two important pieces of material evidence of Allah's creativity at work. His is the command: 'Be' and it 'Is'. The creation of Adam and Hawwa (Eve) was of this order. Out of clay was Adam created. Isa the son of Maryam (Mary), *alaihima's-salaam*, was created by this command in the virgin womb of Maryam. It was a sign (*ayah*) and a clear proof of the command and power of Allah, but many have gone astray and misinterpreted the whole event.

Almost all of the creation, plants, animals, birds, insects and mankind, are in pairs. In scientific terminology the same terms are used for all reproductive processes, egg or ovum and sperm. Most mammals have two eyes, a head and legs. Everything lives for a limited period, a life-span, and then dies. All living creatures eat and excrete. The simple formation of all living forms on variations of a single pattern testify, to those who reflect, that the Originator, the Creator, the Designer is ONE.

THE INCOMPARABLE FASHIONER

Allah has summarised the origin of all living organisms in His statements:

The Seed and the Sperm

"And from water We made every living thing."
(Qur'an 21: 30).

"And He is the One who created from water a human being. Then He has established relationships of lineage and marriage. And your Lord is fully powerful."
(Qur'an 25: 54).

"Glory be to the One who created the pairs, all of them, of that which the earth grows, and of themselves and of that which they do not know."
(Qur'an 36: 36).

"And of everything We created two of a pair in order that you might come to remember."
(Qur'an 51: 49).

"Allah created every beast of water. So of them there is the one which walks upon its belly. And of them there is the one which walks on two legs. And of them there is the one which walks on four. Allah creates whatever He wills. Truly Allah is able to do all things. We have revealed signs which make clear. And Allah guides whomever He will to a straight path."
(Qur'an 24: 45-46).

We have noted the simple unity of basic pattern. The marvel in creation is the great diversity of beings, their colours and shapes, the human beings with their races and different languages. We find it difficult to believe that anyone misses the conspicuous unity of the Creator.

"And of His signs is the creation of the heavens and the earth and the variations of your tongues (languages) and your colours. Truly in that there are signs for the knowledgeable."
(Qur'an 30: 22).

"Do you not see that Allah sent down from the sky water, then We produced by it fruits of differing colours. And in the mountains are tracts white and red, differing shades of colour, and black, intense in hue. And of men and crawling creatures and cattle there are those of all sorts of differing colours as well. They only fear Allah among His slaves who have knowledge. Truly Allah is Almighty, All-Forgiving."

(Qur'an 35: 27-28).

"Or who has created the heavens and the earth and sends down for you from the sky water? Then We cause to grow by it gardens possessing great beauty and delight. It is not in your power to make their trees grow. Is there a god with Allah? No, rather they are a people who swerve from the truth."

(Qur'an 27: 60).

The overwhelming varieties of created beings, their environments and their climates naturally arouse a strong sense of the presence of the Creator in those who explore His wonders and reflect on them. It is natural to believe that for every phenomenon there is an originator; the Originator of everything is Allah. There is no spontaneous evolution or development, neither with nor without natural selection. All is the act of the Creator, the Incomparable Fashioner of all things.

CHAPTER FIVE

The Theory of Relativity

I have selected this title, in an age whose main characteristic is theories, to attract attention to the vital importance of the subject concerned.

The unseen is not a theory but a tangible reality. The true perspective is that of our relation to this planet, the heavens, and all eternity which exists tangibly beyond the seven heavens. This, Adam and Hawwa (Eve), our own kind and our progenitors, witnessed. They lived physically in paradise, ate of its fruits, drank its sweet waters, walked on its land, filled their lungs with its fragrant air, and heard the commands of the Creator with their own ears. When they were driven out of the Garden to the earth they told the story of their misfortune, and it was passed on from generation to generation. Allah revealed the truth of it in His books throughout the ages.

The earth and seven heavens are too small compared to the unseen reality beyond them. There, exist the Garden and the Fire of eternity, as realities not abstractions.

Among His realities are His Throne and His Chair which He has described in the Qur'an: "His chair encompasses the heavens and the earth."

(Qur'an 2: 255).

"And they have not esteemed Him to the true value of His worth, and the earth will all be in His grasp on the Day of Resurrection and the heavens enfolded in His right hand. Glory be to Him and **High** exalted above that which they attribute as partners."

(Qur'an 39: 67).

Beyond the seven heavens there is a tangible reality. The whole experience of humanity attests to that. It is impossible for it to be imaginary. We have a witness of the highest standing to it. He is from our own earth, of our own humankind. He saw the home of eternity in its true light. He returned to our reality with an unshakeable conviction of its truth. The Prophet Muhammad, *salla'llahu alaihi wa sallam*, by the power of Allah ascended through the seven heavens with the archangel Jibril until he reached the Lote Tree near which stands the Garden of the Abode, a real and tangible reality.

"At the Lote tree of the furthest limit, near which is the Garden of the Abode, when there covers the Lote tree that which covers. His eyesight did not swerve nor did it transgress. Truly, he saw some of the greatest signs of his Lord."

(Qur'an 53: 14-18).

After ascending the seven heavens, one after the other, there is the veritable tangible existence in all its magnificent splendour. There is the Garden of Bliss in which Adam and Hawwa lived before the Shaytan whispered to them. Their following his whisper led to a dire calamity for them and for all of humanity, who have been driven from that Garden, with now only one way to return to it; that is by following the path of

The Seed and the Sperm

Allah, His revelations, the last of which is the Qur'an, and His Messengers and Prophets, the last of whom is the Prophet Muhammad, *salla'llahu alaihi wa sallam*.

"And We said, 'O Adam, reside you and your wife in the Garden and eat of it freely wherever you wish and do not approach this tree and so become of the wrong-doers.'

"Then Shaytan made the two of them slip from it and so he brought them out of that which they used to be in.

"And We said, 'Descend! Some of you to others an enemy. And there is for you upon the earth a habitation and an enjoyment for a while.'

"Then Adam received from his Lord some words and He turned to him. Truly He is the Ever-Relenting, the All-Compassionate.

"We said, 'Descend from it, all of you. Then if there comes to you from Me guidance, then whoever follows My guidance, so there is no fear upon them neither shall they grieve. And the ones who disbelieve and deny Our signs those are the companions of the Fire, they are in it dwelling forever.'"

(Qur'an 2: 35-38).

The tangible presence of the unseen is vividly brought alive in our hearts by the sayings of the Seal of the Prophets, Muhammad, *salla'llahu alaihi wa sallam*. The human being is really insignificant in relation to the vastness of eternity, let alone in comparison with the Divine, with Whom it is impossible to compare any one, as He says, exalted is He, "There is nothing like Him. And He is the All-Hearing, the All-Seeing."

(Qur'an 42: 11).

"The Knower of the unseen and the visible. The Great, the Exalted."

(Qur'an 34: 23).

Seeing that relationship clearly and in perspective it is obvious that the human being is rather insignificant. It is indeed horrific to say that the Almighty has a son, or a partner, or is the third of three, or to say of any human being of whatever rank or high standing, that he is a god, or as some maniacs allege that god is manifest in them, or in any sense of incarnation.

Abbas ibn Abdi'l-Muttalib, *radiya'llahu anhu*, said, "The Messenger of Allah, *salla'llahu alaihi wa sallam*, said, 'Do you realise what is the distance between the heaven and the earth?'

"We said, 'Allah and His Messenger know best.'

"He said, 'Between the two of them is the journeying of five hundred years. And from heaven to heaven there is the journeying of five hundred years. The thickness of each heaven is the journeying of five hundred years. Between the seventh heaven and the Throne there is an ocean. The distance between its deepest point and its uppermost is the same as that between the heaven and the earth. Allah, Exalted is He, is above that. And nothing is hidden from Him of the actions of the Children of Adam.'"[1]

Allah, the Exalted, says, "Allah has not taken any son. Nor is there along with Him any god. If that had been the case each god would have gone off with that which it had created, and some of them would have raised and exalted themselves over others. Glory be to Allah beyond what they ascribe. The Knower of the unseen and the visible. High exalted is He above that which they associate as partners (with Him)."

(Qur'an 23: 91-92).

"Truly your Lord is Allah who created the heavens and the earth in six days and is firmly established on the throne. The night covers the day, each pursues the other in rapid succession. And the sun and the moon and the stars are subjected by His command. His are the creation and the command. Blessed be Allah, Lord of the worlds."

(Qur'an 7: 54).

It is related that Jareer said, "We were seated with the Prophet, *salla'llahu alaihi wa sallam*, when he looked at the moon the night of the full moon and said, 'Truly, you will see your Lord as you see this moon very distinctly. So if you are able not to be overcome concerning a *salat* (prayer) before the rising of the sun (*Subh* – the morning prayer) and a *salat* before the setting of the sun (*Asr* – the afternoon prayer) then do so.'"[2]

Jareer ibn Abdullah also said, "The Prophet, *salla'llahu alaihi wa sallam*, said, 'Truly you will see your Lord with your eyes.'"

These sayings are confirmed by clear statements that Allah the Exalted makes in the Qur'an: "Faces on that day bright, upon their Lord gazing."

(Qur'an 75: 22-23).

On the other hand, to clarify this ability to see the Lord and Creator in this world, no human being can see God, Allah, with the naked eye in this world, in his lifetime.[3] I adduce in proof of that the statement of Allah, "No vision can grasp Him, but His grasp is over all vision. He is Subtle, Well-Aware."

(Qur'an 6: 103).

The reality of eternal existence is clear to those of deep conviction and certitude. Any sense of metaphysical mystery is abandoned. It is nothing to do with belief in an abstract, or an imaginative vision but, a reality.

CLEAR IDENTIFICATION OF ALLAH
In the Qur'an

One of the supreme statements from any revelation on the nature of Allah is His own statement which we have already quoted, "There is nothing like Him. And He is the All-Hearing, the All-Seeing."

(Qur'an 42: 11).

Similarly, His words, "And there is not equal to Him any one."

(Qur'an 112: 4).

"And the Creator of every thing. And He has knowledge of every thing."

(Qur'an 6: 101).

"That then is Allah, your Lord. There is no god but Him. The Creator of every thing so worship Him. And He is Guardian over every thing. No vision can grasp Him, but His grasp is over all vision. He is Subtle, Well-Aware."

(Qur'an 6: 102-103).

"He is the One who in the heaven is god and in the earth is god. He is the All-Wise, the All-Knowing."

(Qur'an 43: 84).

"And when My slaves ask you about Me, then truly I am near. I respond to the call of the caller when he calls Me. So let them respond to Me and trust in Me in order that they should be rightly guided."

(Qur'an 2: 186).

The Seed and the Sperm

"Say, 'Call Allah, or call the All-Merciful. Whichever you call, then He has the most beautiful names.'"

(Qur'an 17: 110).

"Allah, there is no god but He. He has the most beautiful names."

(Qur'an 20: 8).

"Say, 'He, Allah, is One. Allah is the Eternally Besought of all. He did not give birth and He was not born. And there is not equal to Him any one.'"

(Qur'an 112: 1-4).

"Allah, there is no god but He, the Living, the Everlasting. Slumber seizes Him not nor sleep. To Him belong that which is in the heavens and the earth. Who is there that will intercede with Him except by His permission? He knows what is between their hands and what is behind them and they do not encompass any of His knowledge except what He wills. His chair encompasses the heavens and the earth; and it does not burden Him the preserving of the two of them. And He is the All-High, the Great."

(Qur'an 2: 255).

He is nearer to us than our jugular veins. Everything is under His power, and He is able to do all things.

"Do you not see that Allah knows that which is in the heavens and that which is in the earth? There is no intimate discourse of three but that He is the fourth of them, nor five but that He is the sixth of them, and not less than that nor more than that but that He is with them wherever they are. Then He will inform them of what they did on the Day of Resurrection. Truly Allah has knowledge of every thing."

(Qur'an 58: 7).

These are all indications of infinite power. One has seen modern toys, for example toy cars, which are so closely modelled on real racing cars. These toy racing cars are monitored and driven by remote control. When you look at the TV you see the real racing cars looking like these toy cars even with their human drivers. You feel that all is monitored by a remote control, just the same as the toy racing cars. I hope the metaphor is clear to show the invisible power and control of Allah Almighty over all things.

Allah, the Exalted, mentions in the Qur'an the confrontation between the Prophet Hud, *alaihi's-salaam*, and his people and He quotes Hud as saying to them, "Truly, I depend upon Allah, my Lord and your Lord. There is no crawling beast but that He takes it by the forelock. Truly my Lord is on a straight path."

(Qur'an 11: 56).

Yet the danger in the metaphor is of course that the radio-driven model car has itself no volition and responsibility for its actions, and this does not extend to the human situation. The human has total responsibility for his actions. The bad of actions comes from the human self. If the human is aloof from the remembrance of Allah, then Allah leaves him to Shaytan.

"And whoever withdraws himself from the remembrance of the All-Merciful, We appoint for him a Shaytan so that he is for him an intimate companion."

(Qur'an 43: 36).

"And We have appointed for them intimate companions who then make alluring to them that which is before them and behind them."

(Qur'an 41: 25).

The Seed and the Sperm

Adam, *alaihi's-salaam*, the first created human being, committed the first act of disobedience by eating from the forbidden tree. This is an example for all humanity, that when they follow their whims and caprices and forget Allah's remembrance, and His law and commands and prohibitions, then they are entrusted to Shaytan. And this too is the will of Allah who has given Shaytan permission to tempt humanity in order to weed out those who do not trust in Allah or have corrupt hearts.

Iblis was ordered to prostrate to Adam at the moment of Adam's creation. That was a sign that Adam and his descendants would be Caliphs of Allah on earth. Iblis, in prostrating to Adam was really to prostrate in submission and obedience to Allah who had ordered him. Iblis rejected this command and he became the first of those to reject belief and trust in Allah.

"He (Iblis) said, 'I am better than him. You created me from fire and You created him from clay.'

"He (Allah) said, 'Then go out from it (the Garden), surely you are accursed, and truly there is My curse upon you until the Day of Reckoning.'

"He (Iblis) said, 'O my Lord then respite me until the day on which they are awakened (from the grave).'

"He (Allah) said, 'Then truly you are of those respited until the appointed day.'

"He (Iblis) said, 'Then, by Your might! I will definitely mislead them, all of them, except for Your slaves of them who are sincere.'"

(Qur'an 38: 76-83).

And the sincere? Those who turn from their wrongs and repent to Allah are sincere. Allah says, "Do they not turn to Allah and seek His forgiveness? For Allah is All-Forgiving, All-Merciful."

Ultra-sound scanning is of great help both to patients and doctors. The internal organs of the body can be seen without the need of invasive surgery. Is that not an indication to us and a reminder to us of Allah's all-seeing vision? He sees everything, in any part of the world, or at the bottom of the seas, or in the stomach of an ant, a fly or mosquito. He hears the sound of their footsteps, or the gentle buzzing of their wings when they fly. Everything is within the reach of His hearing, His sight, His knowledge; over everything He is All-Powerful, and He is All-Wise.

"And there were marshalled for Sulayman (Solomon) his hosts of the Jinn and men and birds, and they were all ranked and kept in order. Until at length they came upon the valley of the ants and an ant said, 'O ants enter your dwellings lest Sulayman and his hosts crush you (under foot) without knowing it.'

"So he (Sulayman) smiled, laughingly at her words and said, 'O my Lord, so order me that I show gratitude for Your blessing which You have blessed me with and my parents, and that I act rightly which You will be pleased with, and enter me by Your mercy among Your right acting worshipper slaves.'"

(Qur'an 27: 17-19).

REALITY IN PERSPECTIVE

Let us put our reality into perspective. Imagine our globe to be a circle and the seven heavens are great circles around our world. Beyond those circles of earth and the seven heavens lie the vast reaches of almost endless space, which the telescope has never probed and can never hope to. None can ever know the end of it but Allah alone. Our globe and the seven heavens which are so spacious to our sight look like a tiny little ball compared to the rest of that vast extension of limitless space. It is those sorts of dimensions that one has to bear in mind when one visualises to oneself the unseen worlds of the Garden and the Fire; the Garden in which Adam and Eve, who were of our human kind, lived and from which they were expelled. So Adam and Eve were witnesses to this reality.

Remember that the Prophet, *salla'llahu alaihi wa sallam*, reached the limit of known existence on the Night Journey (*Isra*) and the Ascension (*Miraj*) at the Lote Tree of the Furthest Limit (*Sidratu'l-Muntaha*), at which is also the Garden of the Abode. (Qur'an 53: 14-15)

These are of the eye-witnesses from the land of human reality to have witnessed that limitless existence and the reality of the unseen eternity and yet honoured us by living among us on earth with certain conviction and unshaken belief.

Allah describes the width of paradise as being the width of the heavens and the earth. Perhaps that is only one of the Gardens of Bliss, so then imagine what are the dimensions of eternity!

Allah, the Exalted, says, "Race for forgiveness from your Lord and a Garden whose width is the heavens and the earth prepared for the people who protect themselves (from evil)."

Similarly Jahannam is ample and spacious and in it live in anguish numerous humans from aeons of existence.

The Chair (*kursi*) of Allah encompasses the heavens and the earth and yet it is only like a small ring thrown in a piece of land in comparison to the Throne (*arsh*). So, we on our vast earth are like a tiny particle in the seven heavens. And all the heavens to the Chair are like coins tossed upon it. And the Chair is, as we noted, in comparison to the Throne like a ring cast in a valley of a stretch of land.

Abdullah ibn Masoud, *radiya'llahu anhu*, said, "A Rabbi came to the Messenger of Allah, *salla'llahu alaihi wa sallam*, and said, 'O Muhammad, we have learnt that Allah puts the heavens on one finger, all the lands on one finger, the trees on one finger and all created beings on one finger, and says, "I am the King."'

"The Prophet, *salla'llahu alaihi wa sallam*, smiled broadly and approvingly and recited the *ayah* from the Qur'an, 'And they have not esteemed Him to the true value of His worth, and the earth will all be in His grasp on the Day of Resurrection and the heavens enfolded in His right hand. Glory be to Him and high exalted above that which they attribute as partners.'"

(Qur'an 39: 67).

Abdullah ibn Umar, *radiya'llahu anhu*, narrated that the Prophet, *salla'llahu alaihi wa sallam*, said:

"Allah will roll up the heavens on the Day of Resurrection and then He will take hold of them with His right hand and say:

"'I am the King. Where are all the tyrants? Where are all the arrogant ones?' Then He will fold up the seven lands and take hold of them in His left hand and say, 'I am the King. Where are all the tyrants? Where are all the arrogant ones?'"[4]

The Seed and the Sperm

This agrees with the *ayah*, "The day on which they will all come forth, not a single thing of theirs being hidden from Allah. 'To whom belongs the kingdom on this day? To Allah, the One, the Overwhelming.'"

(Qur'an 40: 16).

"On the day when We will roll up the heavens like a scroll for writings. Just as We began the first of creation We will repeat it. A promise binding upon Us. Truly We shall do it."

(Qur'an 21: 104).

A more vivid description which shows the relationship of the size of the heavens and the earth to their Creator with all His grandeur and majesty, is given in the following *hadith* (saying of the Prophet *salla'llahu alaihi wa sallam*).

Abdullah ibn Abbas, *radiya'llahu anhu*, said, "The seven heavens and the seven lands are nothing in the palm of the All-Merciful so much as like a mustard seed in one of your hands."

Allah is nearer to us than our jugular veins, and He is near also in that He hears our cries and our prayers. How ignorant of us that we human beings fail to be aware of the tremendous One who holds us in His powerful grasp. He is unseen to us but there is nothing unseen to Him, nothing far from His reach. To Him belongs the creation of every thing and the command over it. Our vision and our other senses are limited. In the childish imagination the Almighty is conceived of merely as a potentate, albeit it mightier than a king or an emperor, being unable to grasp the true nature of the All-Powerful, the All-Knowing whose will is such that when He wills a thing He only has to say to it 'Be' and it 'Is'. Adam was created by this command and so was Isa, *alaihima's-salaam*. Despite the apparent relations of cause and effect this is the true nature of Allah's creation which we witness everyday around us. Nothing is like Allah, the Almighty.

It is hard, from the aforementioned and from the scientific evidence with which we are daily inundated, for us not to realise how minute the human is in the cosmic scale. We look to our surroundings on earth, then to the heavens, and we feel their vastness and greatness. Now, to bring the picture closer to you, if you hold in your hand a small coin, you are looking at it from above and you can see it small and you can see it all. To Allah is the highest example. As has been described in the *hadith* of the Prophet, *salla'llahu alaihi wa sallam*, the whole earth and the heavens, in the hand of the Almighty are like a coin or a mustard seed. With all His powers and Mighty Infinite Ability, beyond our limited imagination, nothing is far from Him and nothing is concealed from Him. Isn't that clear enough? Then see how man is deceived when he declares that a human, a creation of Allah, by the command of Allah, is a person of a trinity, a son of god, or a god himself, how glorious is Allah beyond that! These are very serious allegations, as you can imagine. If the person then claims that he hasn't said these things and that he believes in the Oneness of Allah as we do, then he must believe in all of the prophets, *alaihimu's-salaam* and in all of their revelations. They must believe in the last Prophet Muhammad, *salla'llahu alaihi wa sallam*, and in the revelation vouchsafed to him, the Qur'an. If some make any division between Allah and His messengers then they are the true unbelievers, the ones who cover over the truth.

"Truly the ones who disbelieve in Allah and they want to make a division between Allah and His Messengers and they say 'We affirm some and we reject others' and they want to take a way in between that, those, truly they are the ones who disbelieve. And We have prepared for the ones who disbelieve a humiliating torment."

(Qur'an 4: 150-151).

Shaytan, as is his nature and his commission, is deceiving many and leading them straight to the Fire. Allah, in His highness and exaltation, is very near, and in His nearness He is very high and exalted. Carefulness is a quality of those who affirm the truth. They must be very careful in their conduct and in their behaviour towards their Creator, towards His creatures, and obedient to the laws of Allah. Everyone is the child of his own deeds. One's good and bad deeds return to one. Those whose hearts are sound and at rest in belief will always win through and be saved, sooner or later. It is vital to have a strong will and determination to travel on the right path, to obey and love the Creator with honesty and sincerity. Although we are in time and space and Allah is exalted above these two, yet it is possible to be aware of the almost-tangible presence of Allah with a nearness which is immeasurable by the senses. He gave an appointment for Musa and the Children of Israel to meet with Him at a specific time and place. His presence there also included His conversation with Musa: "And when We appointed for Musa forty nights then you (the Children of Israel) took to yourselves the calf (as an idol) after him and you are unjust wrong-doers."

(Qur'an 2: 51).

"And when Musa came to Our appointment and his Lord spoke to him, he said, 'My Lord show me that I may look upon You.'

"He (Allah) said, 'You will not see Me. But look to the mountain then if it remains settled in its place so you will see Me.' Then when his Lord revealed Himself to the mountain He made it crumble to dust, and Musa fell down in a swoon.

"When he recovered he said, 'Glory be to You, I have turned in penitence to You and I am the first of the believers.'"

(Qur'an 7: 142-143).

Given what we have tried to establish of the incomparable nature of the Divine and His exaltation above all phenomena, is it not a great travesty of the truth to assign to Him a son, a partner or to allege that any human being, whether a prophet or not, is a god or contains god within him? It is not indeed the eyes which are blind but the hearts.

"Say, 'Do you really deny the One who created the earth in two days and do you set up equals to Him?' That is the Lord of the creatures. And He has made on it (the earth) firm mountains above it and He has placed blessing in it, and He has decreed and measured out its nourish-ments in it in four days without distinction for the ones who ask.

"Then He lifted Himself to the heaven when it was smoke and said to it and to the earth, 'Come willingly or unwillingly.'

The Seed and the Sperm

"They said, 'We come willingly.' So He completed them as seven heavens in two days and revealed in each heaven its command. And We have adorned the lower heaven with lamps and a guard. That is the decree of the Almighty, the All-Knowing."

(Qur'an 41: 9-12).

"And with Him are the keys of the unseen, none knows them but He. He knows what is in the land and the sea. Not a leaf falls but He knows it, nor a grain amid the darkness of the earth, nor anything fresh or dry but that it is in a clear book."

(Qur'an 6: 59).

"And you are not on any business, nor do you recite Qur'an, and nor do you do any action but that We were witnesses over you when you were deeply engrossed in it. And there does not escape from the attention of your Lord the weight of an ant (the tiniest particle) in the earth nor in the sky, and not smaller than that nor bigger but that it is in a clear book."

(Qur'an 10: 61).

Suppose that you are a creative person and that you have made a work of art. You know it through and through, you are well acquainted with it. It is 'near' to you no matter where you are. You see and know every part of it. If it has a voice you can hear that voice. You can well understand why the Creator has such a detailed knowledge of the creation and nearness to it.

"In the name of Allah the All-Merciful, the Compassionate, whatever is in the heavens and the earth glorifies Allah and He is the Almighty, the All-Wise. His is the kingship of the heavens and the earth. He makes live and He makes to die. And He is able to do all things. He is the First and the Last and the Outward and the Inward and He has knowledge of all things. He is the One who created the heavens and the earth in six days and then He settled Himself upon the throne. He knows what penetrates into the earth and what comes out of it and what descends from the sky and what ascends into it. And He is with you wherever you are. And Allah sees what you are doing. His is the kingship of the heavens and the earth, and to Allah do all affairs return. He makes the night enter into the day and he makes the day enter into the night and He knows fully what is in the breasts. Believe in Allah and His Messenger and spend from that of which He made you inheritors. Then for the ones of you who believe and spend, for them there is great reward."

(Qur'an 57: 1-7).

"The ones who consume usury do not stand but as the one stands whom Shaytan has driven to madness by his touch. That is because they said, 'Buying and selling are only like usury', whereas Allah has permitted buying and selling and forbidden usury. So whomever there comes to him an exhortation from his Lord and he desists then he shall be pardoned for the past, and his affair is with Allah. And whoever returns (and repeats) then those are the companions of the Fire, they are abiding in it. Allah effaces usury and he gives increase for acts of generosity and charity. And Allah does not love every guilty ungrateful one."

(Qur'an 2: 275-276).

"O you who believe, fear Allah and abandon what remains of usury if you are believers. If not, take notice of war from Allah and His Messenger; but if you

repent you shall have your capital sums; deal not unjustly and you shall not be dealt with unjustly."
(Qur'an 2: 278-279).

Allah, the Exalted, is Great. The seven heavens and
the seven lands are in His palm like one of the tiniest
of seeds, a mustard seed. He is over His creation upon
His Throne, over His Chair, which itself encompasses
the heavens and the earth. Without any likeness known
to us, unique in His Onlyness, His Oneness, Greatness
and Highness. "Nothing is like Him."

"Allah is the One who created the heavens and the
earth and that which is between them in six days, then
He settled upon the Throne. You have not apart from
Him a guardian friend nor an intercessor. Do you not
bring yourselves to remember? He manages the affair
from the sky to the earth, then it ascends to Him in a
day whose measure is a thousand years of what you
count. That is the Knower of the unseen and the visible, the Almighty, the All-Compassionate. The One
who perfected everything which He created and He
began the creation of man from clay. Then He made
his progeny from an extraction of a mean and low
water. Then He perfected him and breathed into him
of his spirit and He made for you hearing and sight
and hearts. How little you show gratitude."
(Qur'an 32: 4-9).

RECOGNISE YOUR DISPOSITION
The intricacy of man's creation is so highly evolved
and sophisticated as to leave far behind the most ad-
vanced technology yet existing or conceivable by our
current visionaries. He is a very highly sophisticated

apparatus. If he looks into himself, actually he has nothing of his own. Consider the eyesight. It works a little bit like the camera. Or rather the camera is modelled on the eye and so it is a rather puny attempt to embody the slight knowledge gained of the eye's workings. The light of an object goes into the pupil of the eye passing through the corneal lens and onto the retinal screen at the back of the eyeball, where the image formed is actually upside-down. By the workings of the retina, the nervous system and the brain, the image is transferred the right way up to the brain where it is seen as a clear and true image of the object. The picture enters the eye, light enters the eye rather than light emerging from the eye to illuminate the object.

"Most of the focusing power of the eye is due to the bending of the incoming light by refraction at the corneal surface. The pupil confines the light rays used in the formation of the image to those passing through the centre of the lens system. The lens then focuses parallel light onto the retina. The eye has an ability of accommodation over a wide range. The eye is perhaps the most fascinating of all optical instruments because of its perfection as a sensory mechanism, as an optical system, and at the same time as a data processing instrument."[5]

"So blessed is Allah, the best of creators."
(Qur'an 23: 14).
Allah's marvellous infinite power is truly tremendous. He moves the lens of the eye into the perspective He wants. He can make the enemy seem little in your eyes, or you seem few in their eyes, as happened at Badr:

"And when He showed you them, when you met, in your eyes as few, and He made you seem few in their eyes in order that He might accomplish a matter that was already done. And to Allah return the affairs."

(Qur'an 8: 44).

Allah, the Exalted, quotes what the Prophet Nuh, *alaihi's-salaam*, said to his people about the way that they saw his followers as despicable, "Nor do I say to those your eyes despise, Allah will not give them any good. Allah knows best what is in their selves."

(Qur'an 11: 31).

In cases of fear one sees the image of what one fears enlarged. The pupil of the eye dilates to admit more light, because of fear and other overpowering impressions. The action spreads to the heart, brain and nervous system; people tremble from fear.

In *shirk* (polytheism), i.e. seeing power belonging to a number of different entities rather than seeing it belonging alone to Allah, then the man of *shirk* sees himself belittled in front of those he takes to be powerful. People are thus made to see themselves as small and insignificant before those of a higher social standing and rank than them, superiors in their employment, doctors, rulers, kings and bank managers and general managers. On the other hand those higher ranked beings see others as little, as negligible.

These are examples related to the faculty of sight. Other examples can be found from the faculties of speech (and the voice), the movements of the countenance and how they relate to the heart, brain and nervous system. These are much in evidence in slave-master relationships, or child-father, young-old and male-female, relationships. It is all held in balance, in gravity and harmony by the Almighty. To every action there is an opposite and proportionate reaction. It is when tears gush out in pain and ecstacy or the eyes glitter in joy. It is in the radiant smiles, with blooming faces, or with angry looks, or in the deep sighs within.

"And do not pursue that of which you have no knowledge. Truly the hearing and the sight and the heart; all of these shall be questioned about it."

(Qur'an 17: 36).

"Say, 'Who provides for you from the sky and the earth? Or who possesses hearing and sight? And who brings the living out from the dead, and brings the dead out from the living? And who manages the affair?'

"They will say, 'Allah.'

"Say, 'Will you not then fear (Him)?'"

(Qur'an 10: 31).

"And Allah brought you out from the wombs of your mothers, you knowing nothing, and He made for you hearing, sight and hearts that you might show thanks."

(Qur'an 16: 78).

Those who disbelieved among the Arabs used to sneer and look with deep enmity upon the Prophet, *salla'llahu alaihi wa sallam*, to shake his composure. Allah, consoling him and protecting his heart from sorrow, revealed:

"The ones who disbelieve almost strike you down with their glances when they hear the remembrance and they say, 'Surely, he is definitely possessed,' and it is nothing but a remembrance for the creatures."

(Qur'an 68: 51-52).

These *ayats* clarify an important point which we should not overlook; that these senses, the eyesight, hearing and the heart's intelligence are means which the human is expected to use and not deny, in his lifetime. They must be used as worship of Allah, and in the ways indicated by the Qur'an and the Sunnah. If one uses them in ways which are against the laws of Allah, then one can rightly expect punishment from Allah, unless He grants one the gift of turning to Him from one's wrong and subsequent forgiveness. One is taken to account for the wrong and senseless acts one commits with severity and punishment or yet with Allah's forgiveness, but one is taken to account for the good and useful acts with reward and kindness.

The *shariah* of Islam is very clear on what is forbidden, for example, the act of adultery, which is clear and unambiguous. Yet, no-one should think lightly of lesser matters of the senses which are not apparently gross violations of the *shariah*, but nevertheless may lead to such infringements. This means that following one's whims and caprices by making enchanting and charming advances to women, flirting with them, or women and girls flirting with young men, that one is accountable for all of these. They can lead to other things. That is why Allah has ordered women to veil themselves and for both men and women to lower their eyes. Flirtatious looks from either party are the foreplay of sexual encounter, and are sometimes considered as amounting to adultery of the senses. When one deviates from the path of Allah one is abandoned to oneself and Shaytan. Misuse of the senses is an action for which one is accountable.

"Does man reckon that he will be left purposeless? Was he not a drop of sperm ejaculated, then he was a

blood-clot, then He formed and perfected and made of him two of a pair, the male and the female."
(Qur'an 75: 36-39).

How terrifying and overwhelming the power of Allah is! For He will leave in error those who choose it, once the heart has become, deaf and blind. From fear of that, the Prophet, *salla'llahu alaihi wa sallam,* used to say frequently, "O Allah, who moves the hearts and the sight, make my heart steadfast in Your religion."[6] He asked that, among other reasons, so that he would not be moved or deviated by the gestures and sneers, by the assemblies and gatherings of the wrong-doers. He wanted Allah to always keep his heart on the right way for he knew that the hearts are completely under the dominion of Allah. The history of the Prophet Muhammad's patience, perseverance, his constant endeavour and his tolerance, is a valuable heritage of wisdom for Muslims.

That focusing and adjustment of the eye, and the all-important inner eye, are indeed overwhelming means to perception, perspective and balance. Those who believe in the mob, or the *people*, see them as great and overpowering. Whatever one values is then seen and heard to be great, sight and hearing adjust themselves accordingly. Sometimes one hears words which are piercing and irritating, but at other times you may feel cool and dispassionate towards them. Sometimes one may not tolerate the murmur of the wind, or the whispering of people, but at other times one finds the roaring of aeroplane engines or the crack of thunder congenial. Sometimes one feels strong and staunch, at other times weak and fragile.

The Seed and the Sperm

The faithful, because of their heedfulness and remembrance of Allah, and because they genuinely fear Him alone and are imbued with a deep conviction of Allah's presence and nearness, see others, the rest of the creation with clarity. That is a gift of Allah, and sometimes He can leave one powerless, one can do nothing and are incapable of acting against certain persons, no matter what one wills or desires.

The Companions, *radiya'llahu anhum*, after the overwhelming victory that was the conquest of Makkah, marched with the Prophet, *salla'llahu alaihi wa sallam*, against Hunain, a small town in the vicinity of Makkah. The general feeling of the Companions was that it would be an easy victory because of their overwhelming numbers upon which most of them sub-consciously depended. Allah taught them a lesson, never to be forgotten, that reliance should always be upon Him alone, and so all their subsequent victories were from their faith in, and dependence upon, Him alone, without hesitation. They were amazed at the stubborn resistance at Hunain, and almost broke down had it not been for the rescue of Allah and His support for His Prophet Muhammad, *salla'llahu alaihi wa sallam*. Allah shook the earth under their feet when they depended upon their great numbers. And He rescued them, when they had almost despaired, and made His Prophet and the Companions victorious. (See Qur'an 8: 10).

"Assuredly Allah did help you in many battlefields and on the day of Hunain when your great numbers pleased you but it was of no use to you, and the earth was straitened, for all its expanse, and then you turned your backs in flight. But Allah sent down His tranquil-

lity upon His Messenger and upon the believers and He sent down troops which you didn't see and He punished the unbelievers. And that is the recompense of the ones who disbelieve and are ungrateful."
(Qur'an 9: 25-26).

"There is no god but Allah alone, no partner to Him. His is the kingship and His the praise. He gives life and He gives death and He is living and does not die. In His hand is the good and He is able to do all things."

The votaries of observation and experiment might be excused for concluding that we are just like machines with delicate, sensitive and subtle, senses and feelings, yet if we admitted that we would have to add that this machine is accountable for its deeds in another existence after death. If there is a pure heart imbued with belief and trust, then all is well; otherwise it is merely a piece of old machinery, yet more garbage to be consigned to the Fire like any other useless material. That looks like sarcasm, but it is a statement of the inexorable facts of the case, whether one is a 'believer' or an 'un-believer'.

We have examined, in a little detail, sight. We could as easily have looked into hearing.

"The ear is marvellously sensitive to the minute quiverings that come to it through the air, and then pass down the tube of the ear and come finally to the delicate organs within. We say that we hear a sound, which means that somewhere or other an air quiver has been started and has reached our ears. We can interpret what we hear because all the tremors are different and we have learnt to know them all. We can tell the sort that is made by thunder or the call of an animal. The ear has such marvellous power that it can sort them all out from each other, can tell one person's voice from another, can tell one word from another, can even tell by the minutely differing shades of inflection the spirit behind the words. The more one thinks about it, the more wonderful one finds it."[7]

Allah, Exalted is He, taught Adam the names, all of them, right at the beginning of history.

(See Qur'an 2: 31-33).

And the brain and the heart we have been given to evaluate and to understand with. As we have seen, we see as we value. From this perspective it is obvious that it is the hearts which become blind:

"Do they not travel in the land and have they hearts with which they can reason? Or ears with which they hear? Because it is not their sights which are blind but rather the hearts are blind which are in the breasts."

(Qur'an 22: 46).

"And We have made for Jahannam many of Jinn and mankind. They have hearts with which they do not understand, and they have eyes with which they do not see, and they have ears with which they do not hear. Those, they are like the cattle, rather they are further astray. Those, they are the heedless."

(Qur'an 7: 179).

"For surely you will not make the dead to hear, and you will not make the deaf hear the call if they turn their backs in retreat. Nor are you a guide for the blind from out of their blindness. You will only make hear those who trust and affirm Our *ayats* and so they submit (in Islam)."

(Qur'an 30: 52-53).

If we follow the rather over-used image of the human being as a computer or a machine, then we can say that, like the computer which only produces what it has been programmed to produce, if one fills the human with garbage he will give out garbage, but that if one fills him with good he will give out good. This human machine however can be destroyed, spiritually as well as physically. Only the human can be turned away from the path of Allah by disobedience to the commands and prohibitions of Allah; by his committing wrong actions such as the drinking of intoxicating liquor, adultery, theft, gambling, murder, telling lies and backbiting. And the undoing of all these is in turning to Allah from one's wrong actions and doing right actions, which cancel utterly all bad deeds and puts all in order. In all of this the vital element is the true knowledge of Allah and belief and trust in Him. It is the crown of all deeds, and without it everything is blown away like the chaff of wheat is by the winnowing winds.

Many people are not aware of the true nature of their constitutions, their dispositions. We have only been created to worship and serve Allah, with true faith, following His revealed laws, the last of which is contained in the revelation of the Qur'an and the Sunnah of Muhammad, *salla'llahu alaihi wa sallam*. We are very tiny in comparison to this finite universe, let alone to infinity and eternity which are beyond measure. We can in no way ever be compared to Allah, the Almighty who, by definition, is not like anything, not comparable to anything, and who created us and this vast existence.

The Seed and the Sperm

So one has to have courtesy if one understands the gravity of our situation. The only possible relationship with the Divine which is open to us is utter servitude and total uncompromising obedience.

The other creatures are also subject communities of Allah as He says, "No creature is there crawling on the earth, nor bird flying with its wings, but that they are communities the like of you."

(Qur'an 6: 38).

Even in comparison with them one is not very significant in those strengths which characterise them; one is not taller than a giraffe, or stronger than an elephant, or as fierce as a lion. It is only that we have been honoured in another way altogether over the other creatures of Allah.

"We have certainly honoured the children of Adam and We have carried them on the land and on the sea, and We have provided them of the good and wholesome things, and We have preferred them greatly over many that We have created."

(Qur'an 17: 70).

It is a privilege, we have been given, to worship Allah. It is done through following the revelations made to the prophets. The privilege of following the last of the prophets, Muhammad, *salla'llahu alaihi wa sallam*, is the greatest conceivable. Allah revealed to him, "This day I have perfected your religion for you and completed My blessing upon you and am pleased with Islam (submission and surrender) for you as a religion."

(Qur'an 4: 3).

And in servitude and submission, we are to be Caliphs of Allah, *khulafa*, "And when your Lord said to the angels, 'Surely I am putting upon the earth a *khalifah.*'"

(Qur'an 2: 30).

We are unaware of our responsibilities to our Creator and also of the abilities with which He has generously endowed us, and the bounties which He has showered upon us. The first intimate and vital aspect of our servitude to Him is our worship of Him, our following His guidance. The end of it is that we are required to return to paradise, from which humanity descended, *insha' Allah.*

"And remind! For surely the reminder benefits the believing ones. And I have not created humans and Jinn but that they should worship and serve Me. I do not want from them provision and I do not want them to feed Me. Surely Allah, He is the Ever-Providing, the Possessor of Firm Strength."

(Qur'an 51: 55-57).

This is the real perspective on existence. There is no alternative but worship in submission and surrender. Allah is not aloof in His highness. To Him everything in His creation is quite distinct, from the innermost secret thought of the human heart, to the sting of a mosquito or the wings of a fly, everything of it is distinct and clearly known. Even in the utmost darkness beneath the soil, He is the All-Seeing. He hears the lowest murmuring sound at the bottom of the ocean or aboard missiles in the remotenesses of space. He is the All-Knowing, the All-Hearing, Who is able to do all things.

We witness in the universe and in ourselves, from the seed to the sperm which are the elements of life, health and wealth, the infinite variety of His creations which testify to the fantastic limitlessness of His creative power. We experience His great favours to us, from the water we drink, the fruits and the varieties of foods we eat, the fragrant flowers and perfumes we smell, the brisk early morning breeze of the dawn, the gentle approach of a midsummer night's evening, to the whisper of gentle winds in the grass at spring, the clothes we wear, the heavy protecting wool of winter and the light decorative cottons of summer, the heavy armour of, once-upon-a-time chain-mail, and now bullet-proof vests for soldiers and police to protect them from assault, the protective fire-resistant clothing of fire-fighters, the beaming silvery moon of the night sky to the hot coppery sun of the middle of summer. All are blessings that Allah has indicated in His book:

"And Allah has made for you from what He created some things to give you shade, of the mountains He made some for you for shelter, and He made you garments to protect you from the heat and garments to protect you from your violence. In that way He perfects His blessing upon you that you might surrender (in Islam)."

(Qur'an 16: 81).

This *ayah* is comprehensive and covers most modern protective clothing, such as is used to protect against chemical weapons, as well as all kinds of shades and shelters. So even the very limit of human culture, technology and civilisation indicates Him and tells of His presence and mighty unlimited power.

We hope now that the picture is very clear. Let no one say that Allah has partners, or that He is one of a trinity, or that any prophet is divine or a son of the Divine. "Surely Allah does not forgive that anything should be associated with Him (as a partner). And He forgives less than that to whomever He wills. Whoever associates anything with Allah has indeed forged a mighty wrong against Allah."

(Qur'an 4: 48).

So in supplication it is good to say, "O Allah, the Most Merciful, the Most Compassionate, O Allah Almighty forgive me," using the names of Allah, the Rahman, the Rahim and the Samad, etc. If one calls on other than Allah, one has lost every good and has been mislead away from the path of Allah, as a criminal and enemy of Allah whose reward is the Fire.

I hope we may all reach the shore safely, in good sound heart, everything in its right perspective. The illuminating words of Allah expunge every darkness, ring resonantly in the ears and reside deep in the heart:

"And they have not esteemed Him to the true value of His worth, and the earth will all be in His grasp on the Day of Resurrection and the heavens enfolded in His right hand. Glory be to Him and high exalted above that which they attribute as partners."

(Qur'an 39: 67).

"O mankind, a similitude has been struck so listen to it. Truly the ones you call on apart from Allah will not create a fly even if they gathered together to do it. And if the fly should snatch away anything from them they would not be able to rescue it from it. Weak are the seeker and the sought. They have not esteemed Allah to the truth of His worth. Truly Allah is strong, mighty."

(Qur'an 22: 73-74).

Bibliography

and Notes on the Text

INTRODUCTION
REPAIR WITHOUT
DESPAIR

[1] Time, 6th May, 1991.
Vol. 137, No. 18.

[2] Keith Moore. *The
Developing Human*, with
Islamic Additions by
Abdul-Majeed A.
Azzandani. Dar Al-
Qibla for Islamic Litera-
ture; Saudi Arabia.
1983.

[3] Maurice Bucaille. *The
Bible, the Qur'an and
Science*, the Islamic Call
Society, Tripoli.

[4] Muhammad Ali al-
Barr. *Khalq al-Insan:
Bayna at-Tibb wa'l-
Qur'an*, Ad-Dar as-
Saudiyyah Li'n-Nashr
wa't-Tawzee'. Saudi
Arabia.

[5] Barbara Schneider
Furham. *Adolescence and
Adolescents*. Scott,
Foresmon. Glenview,
ILL. 1990.

[6] ibid.

[7] ibid.

[8] ibid.

[9] Muhammad Abbas
Nadeem. *Al-Islam*. Al
Rasheed Printing Press,
Al-Madinah Al-Mu-
nawwarah. Saudi
Arabia. 1412 H.

[10] Duane Schultz.
Theories of Personality.
pp 05. Brooks/Cole
Publishing Company.
Monterey, California.
1982.

[11] ORAM et al. *Botany
Living Systems*. Charles
E. Merril Publishing
Company. USA. 1979.

[12] John Paul Brady and Keith H. Brodie eds. *Controversy in Psychiatry.* pp. 3,4. Saunders. Philadelphia. 1978.

[13] Including the face (author's note). See: Muhammad Abbas Nadeem, *The Heart and the Veil* (Arabic). Al Rasheed Printing Press, Al Madinah Al Munawwarah, Saudi Arabia. 1414 H. Although this view of the author's is an acceptable one, it is not the unanimous consensus of the scholars of the Muslim community that the Muslim woman must cover her face in public.
(Editor's note)

CHAPTER ONE
THE NECESSITY OF CONTEMPLATION
[1] Fred L. Whipple. *Earth, Moon and Planets.* A Harvard paperback. USA.

CHAPTER TWO
THE SEED AND THE SPERM
[1] Bukhari and Muslim.
[2] There is no other will than His. We are His creations and so are our actions. Out of grains, vegetables etc., we cook food and bake bread, we make butter from the cream of the milk, etc. This is a possible meaning of "... and from what their hands make."
(Author's note).
[3] i.e. Give thanks for the produce of the earth and for the ability to make food from it.
(Author's note).
[4] James D. Hynes. *Botany* pp 365. John Wiley and Sons Inc. New York, London.
[5] Thomas. L. Rost. *Botany.* Wiley. New York. 1979.
[6] Ibid.

CHAPTER THREE
THE SPERM
[1] i.e. the central portion
of the ovum.
(Author's note).
[2] i.e. the chromosomes
and genes.
(Author's note).
[3] i.e the chromosomes
and genes.
(Author's note).
[4] *Sahih Muslim*, Vol. 1,
Ch. cxxv, pp. 181.
Translated into English
by A. Siddiqi.
[5] Al-Bukhari, *Kitab an-Nikah*.
[6] Maurice E. Bucaille.
*What is the Origin of
Man?* Seghers. Paris.
1983.
[7] Muhammad Abbas
Nadeem. *The Wrongful
Inheritance (or towards a
monotheistic literature).*
Dar al-Rasheed. Al-Madinah Al-Munaw-warah.
1411 H, 1991 CE.

[8] Kaven Arms, et al.
Biology, pp 575, 577,
578. Saunders College
Publishing. USA. 1982.
[9] Ibid.
[10] The semen.
[12] It is the clinging
blood-clot which
implants itself in the
wall of the uterus.
[13] Differentiation.
[14] Gestation
[15] Birth.

Chapter Four
REPRODUCTION,
FATE AND DESTINY
(In Some of the Sayings
of the Prophet)
[1] *Sahih Al Bukhari, Kitab
al Tafsir.*
[2] Al Bukhari, Muslim,
Ibn Hanbal, Ibn Majah,
Al Nasai.
[3] Ibn Majah.
[4] Ibn Hanbal,
Al-Hakim, An-Nasai.
[5] William Shakespeare.
The Merchant of Venice.

Collins. London and Glasgow. 1974.

CHAPTER FIVE
THE THEORY OF RELATIVITY
[1] Abu Dawud and others.
[2] Bukhari.
[3] The author has chosen a viewpoint on this issue which is acceptable but about which even the Companions, *radiaya'llahu anhum,* differed. Some of the people of knowledge hold that it is possible for Allah, may He be exalted, to be seen with the naked eye in this world. For the fullest exposition of this see *Muhammad Messenger of Allah, Ash-Shifa of Qadi Iyad,* P101, Section 5, "His vision of his Lord". Madinah Press, Granada, Spain. 1991.

(Editor's note).
[4] Muslim.
[5] Simon G. MacDonald. *Physics for the Life and Health Sciences.* Desmond Burns, Addison-Wesley Pub. Co. 1975.
[6] Muslim and Bukhari.
[7] William Bragg. *The World of Sound.* Dover Publications Inc. New York. 1968.

Glossary

Allah, the name for the Divine in Arabic, is most often translated as 'God' or 'the God'. The English term 'God' can also be understood as 'god' i.e. any object of worship, whereas the unique name Allah has always been understood, even before the revelation of the Qur'an, as referring only to the One Divine Creator of the universe. The name has no feminine form nor plural.

Arabic Personal Names and Names of the Prophets

   Isa, the Arabic name of Jesus.

   Musa, Moses.

   Ibrahim, Abraham.

   Ishaq, Isaac.

   Ismail, Ishmael.

   Yaqoub, Jacob who is also Israil.

   Nuh, Noah.

   Maryam, Mary.

   Jibril, Gabriel.

   Hawwa, Eve.

ayah a sign (pl. *ayat*) these are the 'signs' in Allah's creation which we are asked to reflect on, but they are also miracles. Furthermore the word means units of the Book, wrongly translated as 'verses', which are 'signs' to reflect on and also miracles in themselves.

Belief is most often used as the translation of *iman*, but *iman*, carries the extra sense of trusting the One believed in, in word affirming that belief, and acting by it.

Caliph or *khalifah* (pl. *khulafa*). The one who deputises in the absence of the ruler or the king. Man in this sense is the *khalifah* of Allah on earth. The historical Caliphs stood in that relation to the Prophet, *salla'llahu alaihi wa sallam*.

deen unsatisfactorily translated as 'religion' because it in our time has been confined to the acts of worship carried out in a house of worship, as well as the 'beliefs' of those who frequent houses of worship. Deriving as the word does from the root signifying 'debt' it has been better translated as 'life-transaction' a term indicating the behaviour of one who realises that he is indebted to his Creator. It includes within it the meaning 'religion' as well as ordinary transactions and behaviour in general.

hadith, is an account of a doing or saying of the Prophet, *salla'llahu alaihi wa sallam*.

Iblis was the name of the original being who, in rebellion against the Creator and out of envy of His appointment of Adam as His Caliph on the earth, seduced Adam and Hawwa to eat of the Tree. He is the ancestor of all the Shaytans among the Jinn.

insha'Allah is said when declaring one's intention to act and qualifying it that one will definitely do it 'if Allah willed'.

Jahannam is the name of the Fire of Hell or a particularly deep part of it.

Jinn are the unseen forces which, like human beings,

may choose to be in submission to Allah or in rebellion against Him.

Ka'abah, 'the House of Allah' built by Ibrahim and Ismail in Makkah for mankind to make *hajj* pilgrimage to and to face towards in their *salat*.

Qaroun is Korah of the Bible, the man from the Children of Israel who was fabulously wealthy and was lured by his wealth into *kufr* (ingratitude) because he didn't see his wealth as the gift of Allah to him but as the rewards of his own striving.

salat the regular acts of standing, reciting Qur'an, bowing and prostrating often known as 'the Prayer'.

    dhuhr both the time of midday and the *salat* performed at that time.

    asr both the time of mid-afternoon and the *salat* performed at that time.

    subh both the morning, after the dawn and before the rising of the sun, and the *salat* performed at that time.

shariah is the wide road a community travels upon whose outer parameters are the avoidance of what is absolutely forbidden, such as theft, murder, drunkenness, adultery and usury, and the discharge of what is absolutely obligatory, such as the five daily *salat*, the fast of Ramadan, the *zakah* and the *hajj* pilgrimage to Makkah once in a lifetime for whoever is able to make the journey. Whoever keeps away from the forbidden and performs the obligatory is within the limits of the *shariah*. The *shariah* in its fullness extends to every aspect of life.

Shaytan is the Arabic term for Satan or the Devil, yet, as usual, the translation must be greatly qualified.

There is no doubt that the Devil in Christendom came to assume the aspect of a great, malevolent deity with actual real capacity to harm. Shaytan is the malicious whisperer in the breast of man whose only power is when man gives him it by obeying him. In as much as his temptation is a test and a trial for man, then Shaytan exercises a function in the Divine scheme, yet man is warned that he is a deadly enemy to him. There are many Shaytans and some of them are of the Jinn and some are from the human race.

shirk or 'polytheism' is the act of ascribing partners to Allah, in the sense of seeing that He, exalted is He, needs other than Himself to manage His creation, or in seeing that He desires that worship should go to other than Him along with Him, or that prayers should be addressed to other intermediaries in order to reach Him. Its reality is to imagine that a number of different powers govern existence.

Sunnah is the customary practice of the Prophet, *salla'llahu alaihi wa sallam*, and of the first generation of Muslims in Madinah.

Supplications

alaihi's-salaam, 'peace be upon him' said after mention of the name of any one of the Prophets.

alaihima's-salaam, 'peace be upon both of them' said after the mention of any two of the Prophets.

alaihimu's-salaam, 'peace be upon them' said after the mention of a number of the Prophets.

salla'llahu alaihi wa sallam, 'may Allah bless him and grant him peace' said after mention of the Prophet Muhammad.

radiya'llahu anhu, 'may Allah be pleased with him'

said after mention of one of the Companions of the Prophet, similarly, *radiya'llahu anhum* 'may Allah be pleased with them'.

tawhid or 'monotheism' is literally 'the act of unifying'. It is to experience and live by the knowledge that Allah is the only reality and the only power in existence.

Unbelievers and **they disbelieve** both translations of Arabic words stemming from the root *kafara*. In its ancient meaning this meant 'he covered over', i.e. the action of the farmer who 'covered', with soil, the seed which he had sowed. Thus some translate *kafara* not as 'he disbelieved' but as 'he covered over (the truth or the reality)' it signifying a conscious rejection after recognition rather than disbelief, as it is ordinarily understood. The Arabic word is often used for 'ingratitude' and this is a Qur'anic usage of the word and to be found in the *hadith* in this sense as well. From the same root is the noun form *kufr* which is thus 'disbelief', 'covering over (the truth and the reality)' and 'ingratitude'.

Usury is the act of charging or paying interest on a credit transaction such as a loan or deferred payment for goods. Almost all monetary transactions in our time have become usurious whether the parties to the transaction wish it or not. Usury is forbidden to peoples of all revelations as well as being highly criticised and disliked by Plato and Aristotle, the fathers of Western rational and scientific thinking.

zakah is the yearly obligation of every Muslim adult, male or female, to give a portion of their wealth, when it reaches or exceeds known limits, to the collector appointed by the ruler. The ruler must then decide on its distribution among the categories mentioned in the Qur'an, such as the needy and the bereft, the traveller and in the way of Allah (*Jihad*).

Index

The Seed and the Sperm